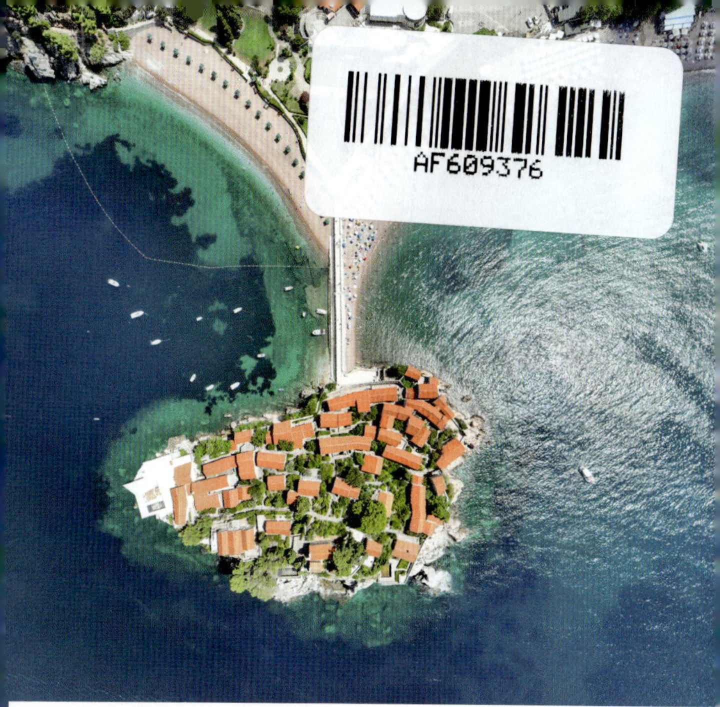

AF609376

The **Mini Rough Guide** to

# MONTENEGRO

# How to download your Free eBook

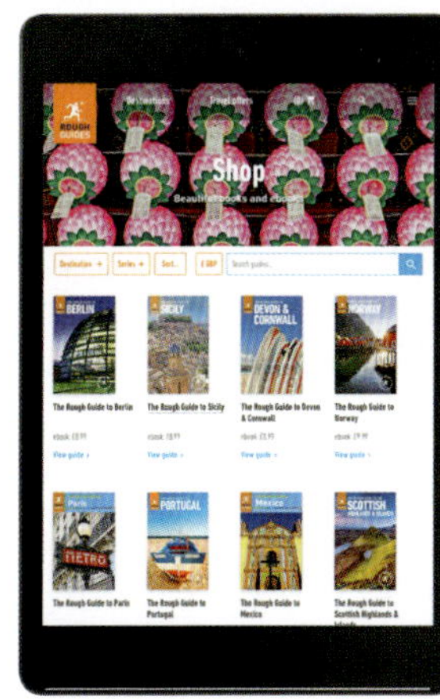


1. Visit **www.roughguides.com/free-ebook** or scan the **QR code** opposite

2. Enter the code **montenegro696**

3. Follow the simple step-by-step instructions

For troubleshooting contact: mail@roughguides.com

# Contents


6 **Introduction**

- **14** 10 Things not to miss
- **16** A perfect tour of Montenegro
- **18** Resort & beaches
- **20** Outdoor playgrounds

22 **History**

34 **Places**

- **34** Podgorica
- **38** The northwest coast and the Bay of Kotor
- **59** The southeast coast – from Budva to Ulcinj

68 Royal heartlands – Cetinje to Lake Skadar
80 Durmitor and the northwest
84 The northeast

**93 Things to do**
93 Outdoor activities
103 Shopping
105 Entertainment
107 Activities for children
107 Festivals and events

**109 Food and drink**

**125 Travel essentials**

**140 Index**

# Introduction

Montenegro lies towards the southern end of the sun-kissed Adriatic, a succession of beautifully preserved old coastal towns lined with beaches which give way inland to soaring, convoluted mountains. Within a surface area of less than 14,000 sq km (5,405 sq miles) – that's just two-thirds the size of Wales – it contains a huge amount that is worth seeing, from beautifully preserved medieval towns to dizzying mountain peaks and enchanting lakes. And despite only having gained its independence in 2006, its history is fantastically rich, with Montenegro lying on a fault line between east and west and having been washed over by some two and a half millennia of successive empires and invaders – from Greeks and Romans to Venetians, Ottomans and Austrians, all of whom left their mark.

## WHAT'S NEW

The Montenegrin capital has just awarded the tender to build a **National Museum of Contemporary Art and Art and Culture Park**. This huge development will constitute the biggest addition to the Montenegrin cultural scene since independence.

Montenegro is entering the final stage of accession negotiations with the **EU** and should join the bloc in the next three years. This will have a direct impact on travellers – EU roaming charges will be dropped and passport checks potentially abolished.

The **gondola lift** linking the coastal town of Kotor and Lovćen opened in May 2023, making visiting the national park even easier.

There are plenty of newcomers on the **hotel** scene. Most notable are the luxurious Mamula Island Hotel in Boka Bay, built in 2023 and situated on its own island in a restored 19th-century fortress, and the Swissôtel Kolašin Resort, which opened in 2024 and is the first luxury hotel to open on the ski slopes in Kolašin.

*A quintessential view over Kotor's Stari Grad*

## HERITAGE SITES

Montenegro's breathtaking Adriatic coast is dotted with a succession of magnificent heritage sites – nowhere more so than the dramatically beautiful Bay of Kotor, a steep-sided inlet surrounded by great hulking mountains, its mouth so narrow that it was once spanned by a huge chain. At one end of this bay, the walled, medieval city of Kotor is a UNESCO World Heritage Site, a fascinating warren of streets and alleys, its defensive walls more than twice the length of those at Dubrovnik. Further around the Bay of Kotor, two tiny jewel-like islands stand offshore, one of them created artificially by locals dropping rocks into the sea to create a platform on which to build a church – to which one evening a year they still come in a ritual procession, aboard brightly decorated fishing boats.

## NOTES

Montenegro has two major UNESCO World Heritage Sites: the beautifully well-preserved, walled medieval city of Kotor and its surroundings on the Bay of Kotor; and inland, the magnificent, unspoiled wilderness of Durmitor and the Tara Canyon. Several other properties have been submitted to the list, including Stari Bar, the historic core of Cetinje and Biogradska Gora National Park. Watch this space.

Further south along the coast, the old towns of Budva and Ulcinj cling to rocky promontories, their fortified walls emerging out of the crashing waves, while the diminutive cluster of houses that is Sveti Stefan has been developed from a humble fishing village into one of the most exclusive resorts on the Adriatic. Exquisite Roman mosaic flooring can be seen in Risan. Both on the coast and inland, there are some beautiful monasteries – among them the Morača Monastery with its exceptional frescoes in the Raška Style, and Ostrog, its white façade seeming to emerge from a sheer cliff. Excellent vineyards carpet the hills west of Lake Skadar and ancient olive trees scatter the landscape around Stari Bar in their thousands, some of them older than the time of Christ, having outlived the empires that have followed since.

## RIVER DEEP, MOUNTAIN HIGH

Whatever the beauty of its coast, it is the wildly untamed and dramatic landscape of its hinterland – its spectacular mountains, stupendously deep canyons, vast lakes and jewel-like mountain tarns, which are arguably Montenegro's greatest, most unforgettable asset – from the unspoiled virgin forest of Biogradska Gora and the huge mountain plateau of Durmitor to the sprawling watery wilderness of Lake Skadar, and the spectacular and remote mountains along the Albanian border.

*White water rafting on the rapids of the River Tara*

## WHEN TO GO

The vast majority of visitors arrive in Montenegro during the European summer holidays (July and August). This is the time when costs and temperatures are highest, especially along the coast. Travelling in the spring or autumn guarantees a calmer, less crowded experience – June and September are still warm enough to enjoy a beach or lakeside holiday. Any time between May and October is good for outdoor activities, the one exception being skiing which is only possible in a short window between late December and February. Montenegro is not a festival-heavy destination and there is little point timing your visit to coincide with events here. Winter sees most businesses shut up shop along the coast and rainy, windy weather in Podgorica and in the mountains.

This landscape makes Montenegro a fantastic destination for hiking, mountain biking, kayaking and white-water rafting – perhaps nowhere more so than in its five national parks, Durmitor, Biogradska Gora, Lake Skadar, Prokletije and Lovćen. All have distinctive features. Across the edge of the Durmitor plateau, the river Tara has carved a phenomenally deep canyon – at 1,300 metres (4,265ft), the deepest in Europe. Lake Skadar is the largest lake in the Balkans, its sun-warmed waters ideal for swimming and water sports. The summit of Mt Lovćen is topped with the mausoleum of Montenegro's great 19th century ruler poet, Petar II Petrović-Njegoš. Prokletije (meaning the 'accursed mountains') is Montenegro's most newly created national park, a succession of lonely peaks along the border with Albania. Montenegro is a karst

*Lake Piva*

landscape, and halfway along the shore of the Bay of Kotor, the largest submarine spring on the Adriatic coast bursts out of a sheer cliff by the roadside and shoots down into the sea.

Montenegro's wild and rugged landscape and national parks are home to an extraordinary wealth of wildlife and plants. Brown bear and wolves inhabit remote mountain areas, though in small numbers and they're extremely wary of being seen by humans (there's a lot of hunting in these parts). More common mammals include the red and roe deer, fox and wild boar, while the country is home to a whole host of reptiles and amphibians, including the Balkan green lizard, nose-horned viper and four-lined snake. The number of butterflies is particularly astonishing, especially the number of rare species the country boasts. Birdlife is at its richest on Lake Skadar (a Ramsar site) and Ulcinj Saltpans, where you can see Dalmatian pelicans, pygmy cormorants, great crested grebes and little egrets, along with many other species. Plant life is equally rich, from tall stands of black mountain pine alongside the Tara Canyon to a plethora of flowers, many of them rare or endemic.

**NOTES**

On 15 April 1979 a massive earthquake struck just off the Montenegrin coast, causing widespread destruction across the country and leaving some 80,000 Montenegrins homeless. This was not the first major earthquake to hit Montenegro – the great earthquake of 1667 also did considerable damage.

When Sir J Gardner Wilkinson wrote of his travels in Montenegro in 1848, he stated: 'The general aspect of Montenegro is that of a succession of elevated ridges, diversified here and there by a lofty mountain peak, and, in some parts, looking like a sea of immense waves turned into stone.' It's a sketch which still rings surprisingly true today.

*A perfect perch in Perast on the Bay of Kotor*

## INDEPENDENT MONTENEGRO

Montenegro held a referendum and voted to become independent from Serbia in 2006, with 55.5 percent of Montenegrins opting for independence, just narrowly passing the 55 percent threshold needed. This made Montenegro one of the newest countries in the world. Much has changed in the years since that date, both in domestic politics and on the international stage. Since independence, Montenegro became the 192nd member of the UN (2006), has been admitted into the IMF and World Bank (2007), its citizens have been granted visa-free travel within the Schengen zone (2009), and the country joined NATO in 2017. However, the main aim of this tiny Balkan state is to be accepted as a member of the EU, a goal it should attain by the year 2028, becoming the 28th member country of the EU.

At home, the overall number of tourist arrivals continues to rise steadily, with almost 90 percent of these being foreign visitors. The country promotes itself as both a beach destination and an outdoor playground with a large variety of attractions that make Montenegro a great place to visit all-year round. New property developments such as Porto Montenegro and the arrival of an ever-greater number of airlines on the tarmac at Podgorica and Tivat are sure indicators that Montenegro is continuing to grow as a top tourist destination. Still, most of this growth in tourism continues to be along the coast. A surprising benefit is that if you head inland and only slightly off the beaten track, you can quite quickly find yourself in places mass tourism isn't going to reach anytime soon.

## SUSTAINABLE TRAVEL

**Undiscovered Montenegro** (www.undiscoveredmontenegro.com) are a UK-based tour company committed to sustainable travel practices. They support local initiatives, and all of their tours have one eye on their impact on the country's environment. **Nikena Eco Adventures** (www.montenegro-eco.com) is another travel company (Montenegro-based) that operates sustainable outdoor tours.

Litter and refuse management is a huge problem across the southern Balkans – the campaign **Očistime** (www.facebook.com/ocistime.mne) works to remedy the problem through petitions and volunteer work. **Recycling** is in its infancy in Montenegro – try to limit the amount of plastic waste you produce by reusing water bottles or bringing your own.

There's a fair amount of **greenwash** in Montenegro (and across the southern Balkans in general) playing to Western European sensitivities about the environment. Always check claims about a business' environmental policies and practices if you think they are being dishonest or exaggerating their green credentials.

# 10 Things not to miss

1

2

3

4

5

6

## 1 KOTOR

This beautifully preserved walled medieval city is a UNESCO World Heritage Site. See page 48.

## 2 BAY OF KOTOR

Spectacular, steep-sided inlet surrounded by towering mountains. See page 43.

## 3 LAKE SKADAR NATIONAL PARK

The largest lake in the Balkans, a vast watery wilderness teaming with birdlife. See page 75.

## 4 STARI BAR

Historic ruins, ancient olive trees and cobbled streets lined with cafés. See page 65.

## 5 DURMITOR NATIONAL PARK

Montenegro's most popular hiking destination is a UNESCO World Heritage Site. See page 82.

## 6 OSTROG MONASTERY

17th century monastery built into a sheer cliff face. See page 81.

## 7 TARA CANYON

The deepest canyon in Europe reaches a dizzying 1300m, and is a UNESCO Biosphere Reserve. See page 83.

## 8 PROKLETIJE NATIONAL PARK

Prokeltije (meaning 'the accursed mountains') are about as remote and gritty as Europe gets. See page 90.

## 9 HIKING

Montenegro has some of the best, and least cluttered hiking trails in Europe. See page 91.

## 10 SVETI STEFAN

This photogenic little teardrop of an island is Montenegro's most upmarket luxury destination. See page 62.

# A perfect tour of Montenegro

### DAY 1

**Cetinje and Lovćen.** From Podgorica airport, drive to Cetinje, visit its cluster of museums, and enjoy your first lunch in Montenegro at Konak. Drive up Mt Lovćen, then walk up the final flight of steps to its airy summit. Drive to Kotor, stopping to try some local ham at Njeguši.

### DAY 2

**Kotor.** Spend the day exploring Kotor's UNESCO-listed old town, visit the Maritime Museum and climb up to the fortress.

### DAY 3

**Bay of Kotor.** Drive anticlockwise around the Bay of Kotor, stopping at Perast to take a boat out to the tiny island of Our Lady of the Rocks. Have lunch in Perast, then continue around the Bay of Kotor, stopping to see the mosaics in Risan. Take the car ferry from Kamenari to Lepante and return to Kotor via Tivat.

### DAY 4

**Costal drive.** Drive south along the coast, stopping to visit Budva's old town and for a swim at Jaz beach. Continue south past the iconic Sveti Stefan to Stari Bar, stop for lunch at Kaldirma then visit the ruins of the old town. Continue to Ulcinj.

### DAY 5

**Food and wine.** Explore Ulcinj's old town in the morning then drive to Virpazar on the shores of Lake Skadar, taking the more scenic road. Join a food and wine tour from Virpazar, stopping at Rijeka Crnojevića for lunch.

### DAY 6

**Lake Skadar.** Spend a day kayaking on Lake Skadar, with a picnic by the lake and dinner at Konoba Badanj.

### DAY 7

**Mountain journey.** Drive to Žabljak, stopping on the way to visit Ostrog Monastery. Have lunch at Koliba. From Žabljak either drive, or hire bikes, for the 8km (5 miles) trip up to Ćurevac, with a short walk at the end to reach a spectacular viewpoint of the Tara Canyon.

### DAY 8

**Prokletije.** Drive from Žabljak to Plav, taking the old road via Mojkovac. Continue to Gusinje and the Grbaja Valley and hike up to Volušnica, taking in jaw-dropping views of the Proketije peaks. Return to Kula Damjanova by Lake Plav.

### DAY 9

**Biogradska Gora.** Drive back towards Podgorica, stopping to enjoy an easy walk around the shore of Biogradska Lake, and later stopping to visit the Morača Monastery.

### DAY 10

**Podgorica.** Spend the morning exploring the Montenegrin capital.

# Resorts & beaches

## DAY 1

**Herceg Novi.** The first stop on this coast-hugging itinerary is Herceg Novi, the first major settlement you arrive at after the border with Croatia. Popular with Russians and Serbs, the town is not Montenegro's finest, but the beaches are worth half a day.

## DAY 2

**Perast.** The next place to look for a parking space is Perast, a grand old city that was once a wealthy trading point on the Adriatic. It's one of the Balkans' true hidden gems and you could easily spend a day exploring its old centre.

## DAY 3

**Kotor.** No visit to Montenegro is complete without a day or two in Kotor, its old town the finest in the country. It's a popular place that gets overcrowded in summer, but a balmy evening in a waterside tavern in Kotor is an experience you won't forget. Many of the visitors you see in the streets may have come straight off cruise ships that controversially tie up here.

## DAY 4

**Tivat.** Upmarket Tivat couldn't be more different to Kotor, its marina and modern apartments a 21st-century wake-up call. The glitzy town now attracts wealthy yacht owners and Montenegro celebrities, but that won't stop you from spending a few hours here on a brief stop.

## DAY 5

**Luštica Peninsula.** If you have had enough of Montenegro's coastal towns, the bucolic Luštica Peninsula that protects Tivat Bay from the Adriatic is a delightfully low key place of small villages and tiny bathing coves, somewhat akin to Croatia's Istria or Krk island. You could spend a week here seeking out all of the tiny *uvaly* (bays), especially on the south coast.

## DAY 6

**Budva.** Montenegro's most popular beach resort is a hedonistic place with more nightlife than most other towns put together. The sand gets crowded in summer, but come here in the spring or autumn and you can have the whole place to yourself. The resort has some fantastic places to eat.

## DAY 7

**Bar.** Not as popular as Budva, the beaches at Bar stretch for over 2km. Stari Bar above the new town is now in ruins, its old streets and buildings gradually being dismantled by the elements but fun to explore.

## DAY 8

**Ulcinj.** You know you are nearing the border with Albania when you arrive in Ulcinj. The language changes from Slavic to Albanian and there's a different, slightly livelier atmosphere on the streets. Ulcinj has countless little cove beaches that punctuate the coastline north and south.

# Outdoor playgrounds

## DAY 1

**Lake Skadar.** Arguably Montenegro's greatest natural wonder, Lake Skadar, which the country shares with Albania, is the Balkan's largest and a major birdwatching location. A few days on its tranquil banks, feasting on freshwater fish and kayaking its clear, often shallow waters are a relaxing and memorable experience.

## DAY 2

**Kolašin.** It's just over an hour's drive from Virpazar on Lake Skadar to Kolašin, Montenegro's top mountain resort at 960m above sea level. Base yourself here to enjoy a few hikes into the Biogradska Gora National Park or the Bjelasica Mountains in general. There's also skiing and plenty of apres-ski in the first couple of months of the year.

## DAY 3

**Plav.** From Kolašin it's a winding, dramatic 72km drive through the mountains to Plav just short of the border with Albania. Plav is the main service centre for the highest peaks in the country, the Pokletije which literally means 'Accursed Mountains'. You can base yourself in Plav for myriad outdoor adventures or dip back in between multi-day hikes.

## DAY 4

**Prokletije National Park.** Those looking for true wilderness adventures should head to this national park to the south of Plav. Shared between Albania, Montenegro and Kosovo, these brooding peaks constitute one of Europe's least explored areas, though they are now firmly on the radar of adventure travellers. With time, you could attempt the 192km Peaks of the Balkans trail (or at least part of it) which does a circuit through the peaks between the three countries.

## DAY 5

**Tar River.** Plav is a mountain cul-de-sac so you'll need to backtrack to Kolašin to start the spectacular drive along the Tara River. Although only around 80km long, the drive will probably take you all day as the road can be rough and you'll want to stop for photo opportunities. The end of the day should see you in your next stop, Žabljak.

## DAY 6

**Žabljak.** This small mountain settlement at 1450m above sea level is the gateway to the Durmitor National Park. It's a bustling place with locals going about their business and hikers getting ready to hit the trails.

## DAY 7

**Durmitor National Park.** Gouged out of the landscape by glaciers, the Durmitor National Park is Montenegro at its most dramatic with gorges of tumbling water, 50 peaks over 2000m and some winter skiing. Most come here for day hikes out of Žabljak where there is plenty of accommodation.

# History

## FROM PREHISTORY TO THE ROMANS

At Crvena stijena, a cave near the modern town of Nikšić, weapons, jewellery and tools have been discovered dating from between 60,000 and 30,000 BC,. Primitive rock carvings in the form of deer and geometric shapes have survived at Lipci, near Risan, perhaps dating from the 8th century BC.

In the 8th century BC, Corinthian colonists settled on the island of Korkyra (Corfu), then from the early sixth century BC they began establishing settlements further north on the Adriatic coast, including Risan, Budva and Bar. These settlements facilitated the spread of Greek culture along the coast.

*Njegos statue, Lovćen*

Also during the first millennium BC, various Bronze Age tribes – known collectively as the Illyrians – played an increasingly important role in the history of the eastern Adriatic. The most important of the Illyrian tribes within the territory of what is now Montenegro were the Ardiaei, notable pirates who grew incredibly powerful during the 3rd century BC under King Agron, and then under his widow Queen Tueta.

The success of the Ardiaei brought them into conflict with Rome, which launched

*Ottoman soldiers*

an attack on the Ardiaei in 229 BC, following which, according to legend, Queen Teuta retreated to the Bay of Kotor, where she committed suicide at Risan. Subsequent Roman attacks led to the complete conquest of the Illyrian tribes, and the establishment of the Roman province of Illyricum.

The most important Roman settlement in present-day Montenegro was Dioclea, near Podgorica, which gained the status of *municipum* in the 1st century AD.

From the 3rd century AD the Balkans, along with the rest of the Roman Empire, were overrun by a succession of invasions, which the division of the Roman Empire by Diocletian in AD 286 did little to abate. In the 6th century the Byzantine Emperor Justinian regained control of parts of the Balkans, though the area remained weak, devastated by decades of war, and susceptible to invasion.

*Ostrog Monastery*

## MEDIEVAL PERIOD

The Slavs began settling in the Balkans during the 6th century AD, reaching the Adriatic coast in the 7th century. Among the Slavic tribes to enter the region were the Serbs, some of whom settled in the area of that is now southern Serbia, inland Montenegro and Kosovo, an area known as Raška. Other Serbian tribes settled at Duklja (Roman Dioclea, near modern Podgorica), where they came under the rulers of Zahumlje (in modern Hercegovina).

In the mid 9th century, in the face of a rapidly expanding Bulgarian Empire, the Serbian tribes of Raška (near Novi Pazar in southern Serbia) united and formed a fledgling Serbian state, which under the Serbian prince Čarslav established increasingly close ties with Byzantium. Raška disintegrated in the second half of the 10th century, with Duklja expanding its territory and absorbing Raška. In 1034 Stefan Vojislav of Duklja rebelled against Byzantium, and in 1040 managed to defeat the overwhelmingly superior Byzantine forces sent to punish him. Duklja now became independent from Byzantium, and in 1077 Stefan's son Mihajlo Vojislav received a royal crown from Pope Gregory VII and declared himself papal vassal. In 1089, the town of Bar was raised to the status of archdiocese. Increasingly from this time, Duklija became known as Zeta.

In the early 12th century, following internal feuding within Zeta's ruling house and attacks by Byzantium and Raška, the balance of power shifted to Raška once more, with Zeta being reduced in power to the status of Byzantine vassal. In the 1160s the Nemanja dynasty came to power in Raška, with the medieval Serbian state becoming increasingly powerful and reaching its apogee in the 14th century under Stephen Dušan.

Then on the 28th of June 1389, Serbian and other Christian armies were defeated by the Ottomans at the Battle of Kosovo.

## MONTENEGRO UNDER THE OTTOMANS

It was during the Ottoman conquest of the Balkans that Montenegro began to develop its own religious and cultural identity, distinct from that of Serbia. During the 15th century the local Balašić dynasty took control of Zeta. They were succeeded by the Crnojević dynasty, who ruled from their capital on the shores of Lake Skadar, then at nearby Žabljak Crnojevići. Though nominally accepting Ottoman suzerainty, Ivan Crnojević continued to fight against the Ottomans alongside the Venetians and others. However Venice soon made peace with the Ottomans (as a reward, they received the cities of the Montenegrin coast) and in the face of increasingly frequent Ottoman raids, Ivan was forced to abandon Zeta's lowland heartlands and establish a new royal capital at Cetinje, in an inhospitable and remote area inland from the coastal ranges, behind Mt Lovćen. Here Ivan built a monastery, which was completed in 1485, and his son Djuradj had the first book printed in Cyrillic by the South Slavs in 1493. However, by 1499 he had been banished to Venice by the Ottomans, with Montenegro becoming just another part of the Ottoman Empire.

In 1420 Venice conquered most of the southern Adriatic coast, including the entire Montenegrin coast, which was called Venetian Albania. Venice maintained its grip on much of the eastern Adriatic

*Nicholas I of Montenegro*

until 1797, although by the late 16th century they had lost the southern half of the Montenegrin coast to the Ottomans.

Ottoman recognition of Montenegro finally came in 1789, under the ruler Petar I Petrović-Njegoš, later canonised by the Serbian Orthodox Church as St Peter of Cetinje. Petar II Petrović-Njegoš, who came to power in 1830, organised the central government and a police force, and is also celebrated as a great poet, whose masterpiece, *Gorski Vijenac* ('The Mountain Wreath') was printed in Vienna in 1847. His mausoleum stands on the summit of Mt Lovćen. Under Prince Nikola Petrović, Montenegro increased its territory significantly, these gains being recognised by the Treaty of San Stefano in 1878, although they were significantly reduced later the same year at the Treaty of Berlin, which imposed a territorial division of Europe more acceptable to the Great Powers. Montenegro's first constitution was introduced in 1905, and Montenegro was proclaimed a constitutional monarchy in 1910.

## THE 20TH CENTURY

Montenegro entered WWI on the side of the Allies, but was occupied by Austria-Hungary. King Nicholas fled the country and set up a government-in-exile in Bordeaux. However, in 1918 the pro-Serbian Podgorica Assembly deposed Nikola and declared Montenegro part of Serbia, with the establishment of the Kingdom of Serbs, Croats and Slovenes (later known as the Kingdom of Yugoslavia) following later the same year. Hitler invaded Yugoslavia in 1941, with Mussolini's Italian forces occupying Montenegro. The Partisans, under the leadership of Josip Broz Tito, waged a remarkably successful guerilla warfare against the German and Italian occupiers, ultimately liberating Montenegro and the rest of Yugoslavia in 1944.

In 1945, following the end of the WWII, Montenegro became part of Tito's Federal Republic of Yugoslavia – which consisted of six republics (Serbia, Croatia, Bosnia, Montenegro, Slovenia and Macedonia) and two autonomous provinces (Kosovo and Vojvodina). The Montenegrin capital was moved to Podgorica and renamed Titograd.

*Traditional folk dancers in Kotor*

With the collapse of Yugoslavia and the war between Serbia and Croatia in the 1990s, Montenegro sided with Serbia. Montenegro participated in the siege of Dubrovnik in 1991–92, and following the war in Bosnia, cooperated in the handover of Bosnian Muslim refugees to the Bosnian Serb Army. The Prevlaka Peninsula, on the border with Croatia, remained disputed following the Croatian War of Independence, with the UN peacekeeping force only departing in 2002.

## MONTENEGRO TODAY

In 2002 the confederation that was Montenegro and Serbia – having maintained the name Yugoslavia following the wars of the 1990s – was renamed the State Union of Serbia and Montenegro. Within this arrangement, the two states preserved a number of joint ministries including foreign affairs and defence, but also exercised a large degree of autonomy. Montenegro introduced the Euro in 2002.

*Milojko Spajić*

On 21 May 2006, under EU supervision, Montenegro held a referendum and voted by a narrow majority of 55.5 percent for independence from Serbia.

The newly independent country joined the UN in 2006, was admitted into the IMF and World Bank in 2007, and attained formal candidacy for EU membership in

*Tourism is the main industry today*

2010. It has distanced itself from Serbia's stance on Kosovo, recognising the latter's self-declared independence in 2008, and in December 2015, Montenegro was invited to join NATO.

The controversial Milo Đukanović dominated Montenegrin politics from 1991 until 2023, serving five terms as Prime Minister and two as president. In 2024, Milojko Spajić became the current Prime Minister.

Montenegro's infrastructure has improved significantly in the years since independence, and tourism has grown steadily. Foreign visitors account for almost 90 percent of tourist overnight stays in Montenegro, with the vast majority of overseas tourism concentrated along the coast. Major tourism developments and the cheap flight revolution of the first two decades of the 20th century put Montenegro firmly on the mass tourism map.

*Flags of Montenegro, EU and NATO in Podgorica*

## CHRONOLOGY

**6th century BC** Corinthian colonists found cities along the Adriatic coast.

**3rd century BC** The Illyrian Ardiaei build a powerful kingdom on the Adriatic.

**229 BC** Beginning of Roman conquest of Illyria.

**6th century AD** Arrival of the Slavs in the Balkans.

**c.850** Serbian tribes of Raška unite against Bulgarian Empire.

**c.960** Disintegration of Raška, expansion of Duklja (Roman Dioclea, near modern Podgorica).

**1040** Duklja becomes independent from Byzantium.

**1077** Mihajlo Vojislav receives royal crown from Pope Gregory VII.

**12th century** Duklja incorporated into Raška (medieval Serbia); the name Duklja is gradually replaced by Zeta.

**1389** Ottoman defeat of Serbian and other Christian armies at the Battle of Kosovo.
**1420** Venetian conquest of the southern Adriatic coast.
**Late 15th century** The Crnojević dynasty rules Zeta from Cetinje.
**1480s** Ivan Crnojević accepts Ottoman suzerainty.
**1516** Election of first *Vladika* from the monastery at Cetinje.
**1696** Danilo I Petrović-Njegoš makes the position of *Vladika* hereditary rather than elective.
**1789** Formal Ottoman recognition of Montenegro.
**1797** Republic of Venice extinguished by Napoleon.
**1852** Danilo II Petrović-Njegoš removes the requirement that a *Vladika* remain celibate, and gains permission to name his own heir.
**1905** First Montenegrin constitution.
**1910** Montenegro proclaimed a constitutional monarchy.
**1918** Podgorica Assembly – King Nikola is deposed; Montenegro declared part of Serbia. Establishment of the Kingdom of Serbs, Croats and Slovenes, later known as Kingdom of Yugoslavia.
**1941** Hitler invades Kingdom of Yugoslavia.
**1945** Formation of Socialist Federal Republic of Yugoslavia.
**1980** Death of Tito.
**1991** Croatian War of Independence; Montenegro supports Serbia, and joins the JNA in siege of Dubrovnik.
**1992** In a referendum, Montenegrins vote by a 95 percent majority to remain part of Yugoslavia.
**2002** State Union of Serbia and Montenegro
**2006** Montenegrin independence.
**2010** Montenegro attains formal candidacy for EU membership.
**2016** Montenegro foils a Russian-backed coup attempt on the eve of elections.
**2017** Montenegro joins NATO.
**2022** The party that has dominated politics since 1991, the DPS, loses power.
**2024** Milojko Spajić becomes Prime Minister.

Perast Bay

# Places

Montenegro's relatively small size – just two thirds the surface area of Wales – makes it an extremely easy country to explore without renting a car, with frequent local bus connections between the capital and the coast, and along the Adriatic itself. Buses inland from Podgorica are less frequent but it's still possible to get around most of the country's main attractions by public transport, with cheap taxi transfers – or, more energetically, spectacular mountain biking and hiking trails – linking many of the others.

The capital, Podgorica, is a modern city built around a historic heart, Stara Varoš (Old Town), home to many of the country's most important cultural sites. The majority of visitors to Montenegro head to the country's coast and the charming collection of ancient towns that gaze at the Adriatic; UNESCO-listed Kotor, overlooking the mountain-framed Bay of Kotor, is chief among them. Head inland to the former royal capital, Cetinje, and Mt Lovćen, then to the unforgettable Lake Skadar. The mountainous interior boasts Durmitor National Park and the dizzying Tara Canyon in the northwest, and Biogradska Gora and Prokletije national parks in the northeast.

## NOTES

The Montenegrin capital hasn't always been called Podgorica. From 1946 to 1992 it was called Titograd, after the charismatic leader of the former Yugoslavia, Josip Broz Tito. There was a Roman settlement – Dioclea, later known as Duklja – just northwest of the modern city, with a town growing in its present location by the Rover Morača in the medieval period, when it was known as Birziminium and then Ribnica. The name Podgorica – which literally translates as 'under the hill' and refers to the low hill called Gorica – first appeared in 1326.

## WHERE TO SHOOT THE BEST PICTURES

For one of the best views of the beautifully preserved walled medieval town of **Kotor**, climb up to the fortress for a panoramic outlook of the bay. Or explore the narrow streets and squares and get in amongst the city for endless photographic opportunities.

The **Durmitor National Park** is known for its stunning landscapes, home to rugged peaks, glacial lakes and lush forests. The **Black Lake (Crno Jezero)** is particularly photogenic, especially during sunrise or sunset. The **Tara River Canyon** – the deepest canyon in Europe – offers dramatic views. One of the easiest viewpoints to reach is at the **Tara Bridge**, but you will need a car to access it.

**Sveti Stefan** is arguably one of the most photogenic spots in Montenegro. It is a tiny island home to Montenegro's most luxurious resorts. Capture its picturesque streets, beautiful beaches, and the dramatic backdrop of the Adriatic Sea.

# PODGORICA

## HIGHLIGHTS

» Around Podgorica, see page 37

**Podgorica ❶**, the Montenegrin capital, sees comparatively few foreign visitors outside the diplomatic set, and has relatively few monuments to attract them. However, it remains the country's capital and is its main transport hub – unless you're restricting you visit to just the coast, the chances are you'll come through Podgorica at some point – and there are a few museums and other things to see, not to mention some excellent restaurants and some of Montenegro's most vibrant nightlife.

Podgorica was bombed relentlessly during the Second World War, meaning that what you see today is mostly unexciting Communist or Post-Communist concrete blocks, with little left of its former self. Under the Ottomans the city had two main quarters, Nova Varoš and Stara Varoš (*nova* means new, *stara* means old) – the former, within the twin arms of the Morača and Ribnica rivers, is where you'll find most of the action these days, from government buildings to boutiques and bars. The **bus station** and adjacent **railway station** are located south of the Ribnica. **Gorica** Ⓐ, a hill on the northeast side of the centre, provides a convenient compass bearing.

The city's number one landmark is its **Millenium Bridge** Ⓑ (Most Milenijum, also known as Novi Most) – opened on 13 July 2015 on Montenegro's National Day – which spans the River Morača on the north side of Nova Varoš. The work of local Professor of Engineering, Mladen Ulićević, it is 173 metres (567ft) long and

*Podgorica*

**NOTES**

There' a small bar on Stanka Dragojevića called Alan Ford, named after the Italian comic strip (first published in 1969), which became enormously popular right across the former Yugoslavia. There's a good book on the Alan Ford phenomenon by Serbian author Lazar Džamić, though it has yet to become available in an English translation.

is supported by 12 cables attached to a single pylon at one end of the bridge, with 24 more more attached to counterweights.

Podgorica has several museums worth a few hours of your time. The **City Museum** **C** (Muzej Grada Podgorice; www.pgmuzeji.me charge), near the Ribnica on Marko Miljanova, has a good archaeological collection as well as icons and folk costumes, and also houses an art collection. The **Natural History Museum** **D** (Prirodnjački Muzej; www.pmcg.co.me/; charge), located across the Ribnica towards the bus station, was established in 1995 and focuses on the flora and fauna of Montenegro. The **Gallery of Modern Art** **E** (Centar Savremene Umjetnosti; www.msucg.me; charge) is housed in the suitably grand **Petrović Palace**, to the west of the city centre, and contains work by artists from the former Yugoslavia as well as Africa, Asia and more.

Construction work on Podgorica's huge **Orthodox Cathedral of the Resurrection of Christ and the Church of the Holy Savior** **F** (Saborni Hram Hristovog Vaskrsenja i crkva Svetog Spasa), which dominates the skyline on the northwest side of town, began in 1993 and lasted for around 20 years. In complete contrast, Podgorica's oldest church is **St George's Church** **G** (Crkva Sv Đorđa), at the base of Gorica hill, dates from the 11th or 12th century, though most of what you see today is 16th century or later. The concrete **Roman Catholic Church of the Sacred Heart of Jesus** (Presvetom Srcu Isusovu) was built in 1969, replacing a former incarnation which was bombed in the Second World War.

The **Clock Tower** **H** (Sat Kula), near the Natural History Museum, is – along with parts of Stara Varoš – one of the few Ottoman structures remaining in Podgorica, and dates from the 18th century. Another is the **Skender Čaušin Mosque** **I** in Stara Varoš which dates from the late 15th century, and was repaired in the 1980s. A counterpoint to the Millenium Bridge is the **old stone bridge** (known as Stari Most or Most na Sastavcima) which crosses the Ribnica at Sastavci, just before its confluence with the Morača.

Podgorica has a surprising number of parks and green spaces, including the old **Njegoš Park** **J** between Nova Varoš and the Morača. The city's main market – the place to head if you want to buy produce from local villages – is known as **Velika Pijaca**, and is located near the bus station. Podgorica's many bars and nightlife are concentrated in the area around **Trg Republike** **K**.

*View of Kotor from Mt Lovćen*

## AROUND PODGORICA

There are several places around Podgorica worth leaving the city for if you're here for some time. The site of Roman **Dioclea**, later medieval Duklija, lies around 4km (2.5 miles) northwest of Podgorica, though a few scattered remains of columns and blocks of stone are all that remain. **Medun**, around

*Forte Mare (or Sea Fortress)*

13km (8 miles) northwest of Podgorica, was a former Illyrian stronghold, and offers some fantastic views over the mountains to the east (these are the Kučka krajina mountains). Medun was also the birthplace of the Montenegrin hero **Marko Miljanov**, a local 19th century clan chief who entered the service of Danilo I and fought against the Ottomans, distinguishing himself in battle and later becoming a respected writer. His house where he was born has been converted into a small **museum** (summer only, charge).

## THE NORTHWEST COAST AND THE BAY OF KOTOR

### HIGHLIGHTS


- Herceg Novi, see page 39
- The Bay of Kotor, see page 43
- Kotor, see page 48
- Tivat and Luštica, see page 57


Montenegro's northwest coast contains two of the country's greatest draw-cards, the spectacularly indented Bay of Kotor, and the UNESCO-listed city of Kotor itself.

## HERCEG NOVI

**Herceg Novi** ❷ is located towards the northwestern end of Montenegro's Adriatic coast, just a few kilometres short of the border with Croatia. The town was founded in the 14th century by the Bosnian King Tvrtko I, its position at the mouth of the Bay of Kotor giving it considerable strategic importance – as you'll soon gather from the prominence of its fortifications.

The old town spills steeply down the hillside between the main road and the sea, in a succession of steps punctuated by agreeable town squares. Approaching from the main coast road, the first prominent landmark is **Kanli Kula** (meaning the 'Bloody Tower'), an impenetrable-looking fortress built by the ottomans in the 16th century, which also served as a prison. In 1966 it was renovated

*Boats at Herceg Novi*

## NOTES

The Herceg Novi Film Festival (www.filmfestival.me) kicked off back in 1987 (as the Yugoslav Film Festival), and is Montenegro's largest such film event. Herceg Novi has a long association with film, having been home to Montenegro's first film production company, Lovćen Film, in the 1950s, and the first cinema in the town opened back in 1920. The festival takes place in August, with screenings of local and international films (the latter in their original language, with Montenegrin subtitles) within the old fortress of Kanli Kula.

and converted into an open-air auditorium seating up to 1,000 people, and today it hosts the Herceg Novi Film Festival and other events.

One of the town's other main fortresses, the well-preserved **Španjola**, lies northwest of the old town, around 500 metres (1,640ft) uphill from the main road along 13 Jula. The fortress dates mostly from the 16th century, and its name comes from the fact that the Spanish had a hand in strengthening and renovating it during their brief hold on this part of the coast in 1538, until it was recaptured by the Ottomans the following year, who completed building the fort.

Entering the old town beside Kanli Kula, a flight of steps descends to the main square, **Trg Nikole Đurkovića**, surrounded by cafés and restaurants. On the east side of the square is the **Clock Tower** (Sat Kula), built by the Turks in 1667, which at the time served as one of the city gates. In the arch below it there's a sculpture of the Madonna (called the **Black Madonna** or Crna Bogorodica) in burnt wood, made in remembrance of the city's founder, Tvrtko I.

From under the Clock Tower, steps lead up to another square, Trg Belavista, at the centre of which is the **Church of the Archangel Michael** (Sv Arhandjela Mihaila), built from the late 19th to early 20th century in an eclectic mix of Neo-Byzantine and

Romanesque-Gothic styles. There's a lunette depicting St Michael Archangel above the entrance, surrounded by finely carved stonework, while inside there are icons made by the Czech painter Franjo Cigler, and a white marble iconostasis.

Southeast of Trg Belavista, the **Church of St Jerome** (Sv Jeronim) was built in 1856, on the site of an earlier church, and contains work by the Baroque painter Tripo Kokolja of Perast. St Jerome is the patron saint of Herceg Novi.

More steps lead from Trg Nikole Đurkovića down to the waterfront, below the imposing **Forte Mare** (Sea Fortress), which dates from the 14th to the 17th century.

At the bottom of the old town, a pleasant **promenade** (Šetalište Pet Danica) extends along the coast, bordered by flowers and

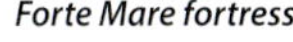

*Forte Mare fortress*

blossoms. Scattered along the shore below Forte Mare are the shattered remains of the old **Citadela**, a Venetian fortress built here which was completely destroyed during the 1979 earthquake and now lies mostly in chunks, either clinging to the rocks or poking out of the waves.

Around 2km (1.2 miles) east of Herceg Novi, on the north side of the main road and surrounded by lush Mediterranean vegetation, is the **Savina Monastery** (charge). The complex consists of two churches dedicated to the Assumption of the Virgin Mary, and another church dedicated to St Sava (Sv Sava, first archbishop of the Serbian Orthodox Church in 1219) on a nearby hill. The smaller of the two 'lower' churches has fragments of frescoes from the 15th and 16th centuries, the earlier ones in the style of the painter Lovro

*Savina Monastery*

Dobričević of Kotor, while the treasury attached to the St Sava church contains, among other valuable objects, a 13th-century crystal cross said to have belonged to St Sava, and an early 17th century reliquary from the Tvrdoš monastery. Many of these treasures were brought to the Savina Monastery in 1693 by monks from Tvrdoš near Trebinje after their monastery there had been destroyed by the Ottomans.

Rising above Herceg Novi, **Orjen** (1,894 metres/6,214ft) is the highest mountain on the Montenegrin coast, its summit a desiccated karst landscape through which the 182km (113 miles) PPT (Primorska Planinarska Transverzala or Montenegrin Coastal Traverse) passes after climbing from Herceg Novi. From here it continues high above the Bay of Kotor to Lovćen, then south to Rumija, and down to the coast again at Stari Bar in the south.

**NOTES**

Montenegro's climate, particularly on the coast, is pleasantly mild. However, according to weather statistics, the slopes of Mt Orjen at the northwest end of Bay of Kotor have experienced some of the highest rainfalls of anywhere in Europe – though, this being karst country, all rainwater rapidly vanishes underground – while Podgorica has had the distinction of registering the highest summer temperature ever recorded in the former Yugoslavia.

## THE BAY OF KOTOR

The **Bay of Kotor** ❸ (Boka Kotorska, or more colloquially, just Boka) is one of the most astonishingly beautiful natural landforms anywhere on the Adriatic coast. A spectacular, steep-sided inlet surrounded by towering mountains, its mouth is so narrow that in medieval times a chain was slung across it to control shipping, its interior opening out into two lobes like the wings of a butterfly. At the southeast corner of Boka Kotorska, the

## NOTES

The spectacular, steep-sided Bay of Kotor is often referred to – inaccurately – as a fjord. Of course, it is not really a fjord, at least in the geological sense – since a fjord is created by a glacier, and there were no glaciers here on the Adriatic coast. Instead, Boka is actually a drowned river valley (technically known as a ria).

UNESCO-listed city of Kotor is the most beautiful town on the Montenegrin coast. A road leads around the northern shore of the bay to the city of Kotor, and there's also a car ferry between Kamenari and Lepante which provides a shorter, more direct route to Tivat and Kotor.

**Kamenari** gets its name from the word *kamen*, meaning stone, and referring to the fine red marble which has been quarried nearby since Roman times. A large chunk of it forms the pedestal beneath Croatian sculptor Antun Augustinčić's 'Peace' monument which stands outside the United Nations building in New York.

North of Kamenari and the ferry to Lepante, the mouth of Boka Kotorska reaches its narrowest point, known as **Verige**, before opening into two lobes. From here the road goes left around the bay, passing **Lipci** ❹, which has some early rock art – depicting two rows of deer, surrounded by geometric motifs. They are thought to date from the 8th century BC.

Beyond this the road reaches the ancient settlement of **Risan** ❺ (Illyrian Rhizon, Roman Risinium), one of the earliest on the Bay of Kotor – where, according to legend, the Illyrian Queen Teuta threw herself to her death from a cliff as she witnessed the defeat of her fleet by the Romans. Very little remains of Risan's early settlement – with the exception of some rather impressive **Roman mosaics**, which are very much worth seeing (www.muzejikotor.me; charge). The mosaics date from the 2nd century AD, and cover the floors of seven rooms of what was once a Roman villa. The most impressive is the mosaic in Room VII (the bedroom of the owner of the villa), which depicts Hypnos, the ancient god of dreams, at the centre of a medallion – the only known representation of this god on the eastern Adriatic seaboard. Other rooms have stylized floral motifs, chequerboard and other geometric patterns.

Further around the northern shore, the road comes to **Perast** ❻, one of the most beautiful spots on Boka Kotorska. Perast has a maritime history quite out of proportion to its diminutive size, and under Venetian rule developed a sizeable fleet of over 100 vessels. Ships from Perast fought alongside the Venetians at the Battle of Lepanto in 1571, and in the 18th century Russia's Peter the Great sent cadets to study at the naval academy of Perast's greatest sea captain, Marko Martinović. Another prominent maritime figure from Perast, Matija Zmajević, rose to become Rear Admiral in Russia's Baltic Fleet. The town grew fabulously wealthy, enough so that in they were able to commission the building of what remains the tallest bell tower on the Bay of Kotor, the 55 metre (180ft) campanile of the **Church of St Nicholas** (Sv Nikola) – at a cost of over 50,000 gold ducats. These days the elegant 17th and 18th century palaces from Perast's heyday make for a pleasant backdrop to a memorable dinner on the waterfront, overlooking the Bay of

*The dramatic Bay of Kotor*

Kotor. The **Town Museum** (Muzej Grada Perasta; www.muzejikotor.me; charge), located in the 17th century Bujović Palace, tells the story of the town's rich maritime history.

Offshore from Perast there are two tiny islands, one home to the Benetictine **Monastery of St George** ❼ (Sv Đorđe), the other known as **Our Lady of the Rocks** ❽ (Gospa od Škrpjela) after the small chapel there.

Gospa od Škrpjela is built on an artificial island, made by locals who dumped rocks and scuttled small boats filled with stones around a small rock or reef, until it grew to a size they could build on. A chapel was built here in 1630, then in the 18th century this was enlarged into a church, and the octagonal dome added. The interior of the church contains 68 paintings by the Baroque

*The Church of St Nicholas towers over Perast*

painter Tripo Kokolja, who was born in Perast. There is a small museum attached to the church.

There are various legends attached to the island. One says that it grew from a tradition of local seamen laying a rock here when returning from a successful voyage, and that the Madonna of the Rocks was later seen on top. Whatever its origins, it made enough of an impression on the 19th century Swiss painter Böcklin that he used it as a model for his well-known (and rather spooky) painting *The Isle of the Dead*, which now hangs in the Metropolitan Museum of Art in New York.

***The Monastery of St George Island***

Each year on the 22nd of July, in a tradition known as **Fašinada**, a ritual procession of colourfully decorated boats sets off around the island of Gospa od Škrpjela at dusk.

The monastery on the nearby island of Sv Đorđe – this one natural rather than artificial – dates from the 17th century. Among those buried on the island is Marko Martinović, Perast's greatest sea captain. Small boats head out to the two islands from the waterfront in Perast.

East from Perast, the road passes through **Dobrota** – another important maritime town, which during the 18th century had the largest number of ships in the Bay of Kotor – before arriving at Kotor.

Continuing west along the southern shore of the Bay of Kotor, the road arrives in the village of **Prčanj** – which has a surprisingly large church, the 18th century **Church of the Birth of Our Lady** (Rođenje Bogorodice), a hint of the village's former wealth and prominence.

## KOTOR

The walled, medieval city of **Kotor** ❾ sits at the southeast corner of the Bay of Kotor, an irregularly shaped triangle of terracotta-tiled rooftops, bordered by the steep, craggy foothills of Lovćen, the River Škurda and the sea. Kotor is arguably the most richly multilayered and fascinating city in Montenegro, the one place you simply cannot and should not miss.

*Lively streets of Kotor*

Kotor is an UNESCO World Heritage Site, or more accurately it's part of one – the Natural and Culturo-Historical Region of Kotor, to give it its full title, was inscribed on the UNESCO list in 1979, one of two UNESCO-listed sites in Montenegro (the other being Durmitor National Park). Along with the city of Kotor itself, the site encompasses several locations around the Bay of Kotor. These locations include Dobrota (which these days seems like an attractive northern 'suburb' of Kotor, though it was once completely separate), the

*Kotor city wall fortifications*

ancient towns of Risan, Kostanjica and Perast, and the tiny islets of Sveti Djordje (St George) and Our Lady of the Rocks (Gospa od Škrpjela). The UNESCO-listing followed the devastating earthquake which struck Montenegro earlier the same year, with repair of the serious damage to several monuments in Kotor financed in part through UNESCO.

Kotor was an Illyrian stronghold (then known as Acruvium) before it was captured by the Romans, who built a fort here. Later, in the 6th century, the Byzantine emperor Justinian built a fortress above the town. Most of the extensive and elaborate fortifications which you see surrounding Kotor today, however, were built by the Venetians, to whom the city belonged for some four centuries, from 1420 to 1797. It is these medieval walls, perhaps more than anything else, which give the city its most familiar character.

*Ruins of St John's Fort*

Kotor's medieval city walls stretch for around 4.5km (2.8 miles) (that's more than twice as long as the famous walls of Dubrovnik, for those counting), running up over the crags above the old town to the Fortress of St John (Sv Ivan), and in places reaching up to 20 metres (65ft) high and 10 metres (33ft) thick.

The best way to appreciate the city's sprawling fortifications, and the layout of the old town itself, is to hike up to **St John's Fort** Ⓐ – an easy 30 minute walk up the steep slopes behind the old town (though bear in mind it can be relentlessly hot in the summer and there's very little shade, so make sure you carry a bottle of water and take a sunhat). The start of the path (charge) is hidden away in an alley behind the little church of St Mary of the River, in the northeast corner of the old town. From here a broad, clear path climbs along the line of the ancient stone walls, with impressive views over the old town below and the Bay of Kotor beyond. Part way up is the **Chapel of Our Lady of Health** (Gospe od Zdravlja), with its domed bell tower. The chapel was built by survivors of the plague, and was used by troops stationed in the upper fort. The somewhat motley remains of St John's Fort itself sit at an elevation of 266 metres (873ft), and command good views of the Bay of Kotor. Just below the fort, a large hole in a section of the walls leads down to the little church of St George (Sveti Đorđe), standing abandoned beside a lone cypress tree and tucked below stupendous crags. The broad stone steps zigzagging up past this church lead from the North Gate of the old town far below, all the way up to Krstac on the old road to Cetinje. This was the so-called 'Ladder of Cattaro', a mule track built before the modern road.

The triangular wedge of Kotor's old city core consists of a loosely connected series of open squares and a jumble of winding, cobbled streets and alleys. Some of the latter get surprisingly narrow – one of them so much so that it's called *Pusti me da prođem*, meaning 'Let me pass'. There are three main entrances to the old town, the Sea Gate (the main one), the North Gate and the South Gate.

The main square as you enter from the Sea Gate is **Trg od Oružja** (Square of Weapons) **B**, which – as the name implies – was

*Cathedral of St Tryphon*

*Evening in the Square of Weapons*

formerly the location of the city arsenal. These days the square is awash with outdoor seating and tables for a plethora of cafés, but the old arsenal building still stands, in the northeast corner. Like the Square of Weapons, most of the city's other squares have names which similarly refer to their main use at some earlier point in history – Trg od Mlijeka (Square of Milk), Trg od Brašna (Square of Flour), and so on. Lining Trg od Oružja along its southwest side is the 17th century **Duke's Palace** Ⓒ, at one end of which is the former theatre built by the French in 1810, when Kotor was part of Napoleon's Illyrian Provinces (it's now part of the Hotel Cattaro). Also on Trg od Oružja is the 17th century **Clock Tower** Ⓓ (the clock itself dates from the 19th century).

Aside from its walls, Kotor's main historical landmark is the **Cathedral of St Tryphon** Ⓔ (Katedrala Sv Tripuna; charge), an outstanding example of Romanesque architecture built in 1166. The cathedral was severely damaged during the huge earthquake of 1667, including the bell towers and part of the façade, which flattened a few of the surrounding buildings when they collapsed, and had to be rebuilt, giving them their present-day, Baroque style. The large rosette window above the entrance portal with details in Gothic-Renaissance style also dates from these later restorations. The interior of the cathedral is a three-nave basilica, the highlight of which is the three-tiered ciborium above the main altar, dating from the 14th century and carved in Romanesque-Gothic style with scenes from the life of St Tryphon. Fragments of frescoes dating from the 14th century have been discovered in the cathedral interior, and there are paintings by the Kotor-born Renaissance painter Marin Lovro Dobričević, together with Tripo Kokolj, Paolo Veroveza and other masters. Also look out for the 15th century gold altarpiece (on the wall of the apse) by local goldsmiths, with the figures of Christ, the Virgin, St John the Baptist and St Tryphon along with other saints. Inscribed on the two monumental bell towers which frame the cathedral entrance are the dates 809 and 2009, referring to the 12th centenary of the founding of an earlier, much smaller church, on the foundations of which the cathedral was built. St Tryphon is the city's patron saint.

*St Luke's Church*

*Kotor old town*

The old town also contains several smaller churches. Perhaps most beautiful among these is **St Luke's Church** **F** (Sv Luka), built in 1195 in Romanesque style – and which, alone in Kotor, has somehow managed to survive the many earthquakes which have since rocked the city (1667 and 1979 in particular), largely unscathed. The church was originally Roman Catholic, then later became Orthodox, and has two altars, serving inhabitants of the city of both these faiths (a not-unusual arrangement). The walls were once decorated with frescoes, only fragments of which survive. There is an inscription by the founder on the western façade. Elsewhere, **St Mary's Church** **G** (Sv Marija) was built in 1221 on the foundations of an early Episcopal basilica, perhaps dating from the sixth century. Fragments of a baptistery from this earlier church were discovered during repairs which followed the 1979 earthquake, and there are also fragments of 17th century frescoes as well as relics of Saint Ozana. **St Clare's Church** **H** (Sv Klara) is part of an 18th century Franciscan monastery, built on the site of an earlier Benedictine nunnery, and contains an impressive Baroque altar. **St Michael's Church** **I** (Sv Mihailo) dates from the 14th or 15th century, and was built on the site of an earlier church following one of Kotor's earthquakes. Today the interior houses a modest lapidarium.

The **Maritime Museum** **J** (Pomorski Muzej; www.museum-maritimum.com; charge) is housed in the 18th century Baroque Grgurina Palace, on Trg Bokeljske. The museum has excellent displays paying homage to the city's long and remarkably rich maritime heritage, along with weaponry and an ethnographic collection. The main exhibition floor is on the first floor, and it's here that you'll find displays which tell the story of the city's 'golden age' in terms of maritime history – in paintings, documents and models of ships.

Other notable buildings once belonging to Kotor's noble families include the **Pima Palace** **K**, which was built after the 1667 earthquake in Renaissance and Baroque style, its elaborate railings the work of local blacksmiths; and the Gothic **Drago Palace**

*Exhibits in the Maritime Museum*

which dates from the 14th and 15th centuries and therefore like much else had to be rebuilt after the 1667 and 1979 earthquakes. The **Bishopric** also occupies a building formerly belonging to the Drago family. Also worth hunting out is the elegant Baroque **Karampana Fountain** – once the only source of drinking water in the old town – which dates from the 17th or 18th century and is surrounded by some beautiful wrought iron railings.

Kotor has a lively outdoor **market** Ⓛ, which stretches along the exterior of the walls, by the waterfront, with stalls selling locally-grown fruit and vegetables, home-made wine and cheeses, and glisteningly fresh fish.

The town also has several festivals. Particularly colourful is Boka Night, held on the third Saturday in August, during which an

*Choosing fresh fruit at Kotor's market*

illuminated flotilla of boats passes in front of the old town. There's also KotorArt (www.kotorart.me) in June and July, and the Sea Rock Festival in June.

The bus station, located just south of the old town, has regular services up and down the coast as well as inland to Podgorica and beyond. If you're cycling, be aware that the main road to Tivat and Budva leads through a tunnel, which is not particularly well-suited for bikes.

*Pima Palace*

## TIVAT AND LUŠTICA

West of Kotor beyond the hill of Sv Ilija, lies **Tivat** ⑩, a small coastal town on the shore of the Bay of Tivat. In the past two decades, Tivat has been at the centre of one of Montenegro's most high profile new development projects, **Porto Montenegro**. The new marina created through this project boasts 450 berths ranging from 12 metres (39ft) to 250 metres (820ft), upmarket hotels, shops and restaurants. Away from the super-yachts, Tivat's **City Park**, founded at the end of the 19th century, remains a pleasantly green oasis, filled with exotic and subtropical plants brought back from around the world by local merchants and sea captains. In the centre of Tivat, the Renaissance **Buća Palace** now houses an art gallery (www.czktivat.me, charge), with exhibitions organized by the Tivat Cultural Centre. Tivat has plenty of beaches – though finding space on them in the height of summer is sometimes a challenge.

*Beach views of the Bay of Kotor*

It's only a 15-minute walk north from Porto Montenegro to **Donja Lastva**, which has managed to retain something of the air of a small fishing village. A road leads up into the hills behind the village, to **Gornja Lastva** (*gornja* means 'upper', *donja* 'lower'), its old stone houses looking out over the Bay of Tivat. The surrounding area is good for walking and cycling, for those who want to escape the buzz of Porto Montenegro for a while without straying too far from the coast.

South of Tivat, past the airport, is **Solila** – a large saltwater lagoon, which is a good area for bird watching. You can sometimes see flamingos here. Beyond this, the **Luštica Peninsula** stretches westwards, forming one of the arms which, along with the Prevlaka peninsula on the border with Croatia, enclose the entrance to the Bay of Kotor. Largely undeveloped until quite recently, with plenty of hidden coves perfect for swimming, Luštica is the site of a large new luxury property development complete with 18-hole golf course, on the southeast coast of the peninsula at Trašte Bay. The small, relatively sheltered beach of Pržno here is popular with families.

Out in the sea off the tip of Luštica is **Mamula**, a circular fortress built by the Austrians during the 19th century, which during the Second World War was used by Mussolini as a concentration camp, where many prisoners were brutally tortured and starved. In 2016 the Montenegrin government made the highly controversial decision to approve plans for Mamula to be converted into a luxury resort, despite objections from the families of former prisoners.

# THE SOUTHEAST COAST – FROM BUDVA TO ULCINJ

## HIGHLIGHTS


- Budva, see page 59
- The Budva Riviera, see page 62
- Bar, see page 64
- Ulcinj, see page 65


South of Kotor, the coast road runs past the hugely popular Budva and the bijou Sv Stefan, to the port of Bar and then Ulcinj with its mainly Albanian population.

## BUDVA

**Budva** ⓫ is the undisputed summer party capital of Montenegro, its waterfront

### NOTES

Some say that Budva was founded by King Cadmus of Thebes and his wife Harmonia, who were later both turned into serpents – although others tell that it was Risan, not Budva, where this took place.

and beaches turning into a unbroken succession of clubs during the summer months. However, look beyond the cocktail bars and the blare of turbo-folk, and you'll find that the history of Budva is very long indeed. Founded by Corinthian settlers from Corfu around the 4th century BC, Budva was part of Roman Illyricum by the 2nd century BC, and when Diocletian divided the Roman Empire into Western and Eastern administrative units, the division of the two ran through Budva. During the Venetian period, Budva's fortifications included walls and six towers, but these were destroyed in the great earthquake of 1667.

Budva's attractive **old town** (Stari grad) sits on a small rocky promontory, a warren of narrow alleys lined with cafés, boutiques and souvenir shops, much of which had to be restored following

*Budva's old town*

the devastating 1979 earthquake. The massive **Citadel** (first mentioned in the early 15th century) provides a suitably grand and atmospheric backdrop to Budva's **City of Theatre Festival** (www.gradteatar.me) in July, and the **City Museum** (Muzej grada Budve; www.muzejiigalerijebd.me; charge) has a good archaeological collection, including finds from the ancient Greek and Roman necropolis at Budva (discovered during the construction of the Hotel Avala in the 1930s) – gold jewellery, glass and ceramics, silver dishes, weapons (among them a well-preserved Illyrian bronze helmet) and other artifacts. There's also a **Modern Gallery** (Moderna Galerija Budva; www.muzejiigalerijebd.me; charge) which began its life in 1972 with a collection of Expressionist works by artists from the former Yugoslavia. The **Church of St John** (Sv Ivan) was a cathedral until 1828, when the Diocese of Budva was abolished. Damaged during the 1667 earthquake it was rebuilt several times, and may have been built on the site of an earlier church, which perhaps dated from as early as the 7th century. The bell tower dates from 1867. The smaller **Church of the Holy Trinity** dates from 1804. At the southwest corner of the old town, the little **Church of St Mary in Punta** (Sv Marija) is one of the earliest in Budva, dating from around 840 and originally part of a Benedictine monastery. Occasional concerts and exhibitions are held here in the summer.

## NOTES

Turbo-folk is a blend of traditional Serbian folk music and modern pop – usually played as loud as possible and for many foreign visitors to Montenegro, something of an acquired taste. The term turbo-folk was first coined by Montenegrin singer Rambo Amadeus. If there's one place in Montenegro where you're most likely to be subsumed by an unrelenting barrage of turbo-folk, it's Budva.

**Beaches** stretch along the coast on either side of the old town and marina – Slovenska Beach (Slovenska plaža) to the east, followed beyond the Zavala headland by Bečići Beach (Bečićka plaža, good for families with young children); Mogren Beach to the west (consisting of two halves connected by a tunnel); and most popularly, **Jaz Beach** which is located around 4km (2.5 miles) west of Budva, and is where the large Sea Dance Festival (www.seadancefestival.me) takes place in July. Boats head out to **St Nikola Island** (Sv Nikola, but known locally as Skolj), just offshore from Budva, which has three beaches – many locals also swim out (it takes around an hour each way). The bus station, which has frequent services up and down the coast as well as inland to Podgorica and Cetinje, is in the modern town of Budva, which forms an arc behind Slovenska Beach.

On the hillside far above Budva, just off the road which zigzags up towards Cetinje and Podgorica, the ruined Austro-Hungarian fort of **Kosmač** was once the southernmost fortress in the Habsburg Empire.

## NOTES

The Belgrade-Bar Railway follows a spectacular route through Montenegro, negotiating the mountainous landscape via a succession of tunnels and viaducts. At the time it was built in the mid-1970s, the 200 metre (656ft) -high Mala Rijeka Viaduct north of Podgorica was the highest railway bridge in the world.

## THE BUDVA RIVIERA

Stretching south from Budva, the so-called Budva Riviera includes the iconic Sv Stefan and the equally popular Petrovac na Moru. **Sv Stefan** ⓬ – a perfect little cluster of tiled roofs on a tiny island, connected to the mainland by a stone causeway built onto a spit of shingle – was once a sleepy fishing village fortified against the Turks, but was developed into an

*Sv Stefan island on the Budva Riviera*

upmarket resort in the 1960s, where guests included the likes of Sophia Loren, Orson Welles, Richard Burton and Elizabeth Taylor. In 2011 it re-opened after a complete makeover as part of the Aman Hotel chain, and is now Montenegro's most exclusive resort (you can't even get onto the island if you're not staying there), with eye-watering prices to match. There are beaches on the mainland either side of Sv Stefan – one of the nicest and least crowded is at **Pržno**, a little further north (not to be confused with the other beach called Pržno, near Tivat), which is popular with families.

There was a settlement at **Petrovac na Moru** ⓭ (meaning Petrovac on the sea) during the Roman period, and mosaic flooring from the 3rd or 4th century AD has been uncovered here. **Kaštel Lastva**, the fortress above the jetty and small harbour, was built by the Venetians in the 16th century. Next to this they built a quarantine house, the **Lazaret**. These days it all makes for a pleasant backdrop to the cafés and seafood restaurants dotted along the waterfront, especially during Petrovac Night, the large traditional fisherman's festival in August. Petrovac Beach (Petrovačka plaža) gets enormously busy in season. The smaller Lučice Beach, a 10-minute walk southeast of town, was once upon a time a quieter alternative, though these days it seems to be catching up with Petrovac Beach.

## BAR

**Bar** ⓮ is an ancient settlement (Roman Antibaris), and in 1089 was raised to the status of archdiocese, although these days it is known mainly as a busy port and the terminus of the Belgrade-Bar railway. The **Bar Regional Museum** (Zavičajni muzej Bar; http://kulturnicentarbar.me; charge) is housed in the renovated former summer palace of King Nikola (Dvorac Kralja Nikole), built in 1885 by the architect Josip Slade and once surrounded by lush sub-tropical

### ANCIENT TREES AND OLIVE OIL

The area around Bar has a long history of the cultivation of olive trees, and some of the trees in this area are very, very old – more than 10,000 of these original ancient trees survive, looking suitably gnarled and in many cases well over 1,000 years old. One tree in the village of Mirovica near Stari Bar is believed to be over 2,000 years old, and may be the oldest tree in Europe. A small annual festival (called Meeting Under the Old Olive Tree) in Mirovica celebrates children's poetry in November. Today, olive cultivation continues to be a strong local tradition – there are more than 1,700 olive growers in the Bar area, and 12 mills as well as traditional family presses. The olive cultivated here is the indigenous *Žutica* species, producing fantastically rich olive oils as well as soaps and cosmetics, all of which can be bought locally, especially at the Maslinijada Festival, which takes place in Stari Bar in November.

and Mediterranean gardens, and has archaeological and ethnographic displays.

Five kilometres (3 miles) east of Bar on a hill called Londža is the fortified medieval settlement of **Stari Bar** ⓯, founded by the Byzantine Emperor Justinian in the 6th century, on a site which had previously been an Illyrian hill fort. It's a wonderful site, bristling with walls and towers and old churches, partly overgrown. The street beside the old town is dotted with restaurants and cafés, making it a perfect spot to linger.

*The town of Ulcinj*

## ULCINJ

Around 25km (15.5 miles) southeast of Bar is the city of **Ulcinj** ⓰. Settled by the Illyrians and Greeks in the 5th century BC (although legend has it that Ulcinj was founded by the Colchians, while they were pursuing the Argonauts who had made off with the Golden Fleece), it later became Roman Olcinium, and in the 14th century was ruled by the Balšić family. Although briefly under Venice, Ulcinj fell to the Ottomans in 1571, and remained an Ottoman possession for over 300 years. The population of Ulcinj is around 70 percent Albanian and 70 percent Muslim.

The **old town** is built on a rocky promontory, its massive fortifications having gradually been built and rebuilt by successive rulers for some two and a half millennia. The little **Church-Mosque** in the old town was built by the Venetians as the Church of St Mary in

## THE PIRATES OF ULCINJ

Ulcinj's most infamous pirate was a certain Lika Ceni, who was responsible for sinking a ship of pilgrims on its way to Mecca, for which the Ottoman sultan put a bounty on his head. However, around the same time another pirate named Lembro also incurred the wrath of the sultan, who then rather cunningly offered to pardon Lika if he would kill Lembro – which he did, and as well as being pardoned (and pocketing a large reward) he was given the rank of captain.

the early 16th century, then converted into the Mosque of Sultan Selim II following the Ottoman conquest of 1571. It now houses the **Museum of Ulcinj** (Zavičajni muzej; charge), which has a good collection of local archaeological finds.

The **Orthodox Cathedral of St Nicholas** (Sv Nikola), near the old town, dates from the late 19th century – it was built on the site of a mosque, which in turn had been built on the site of a monastery. The **Pasha Mosque**, also near the old town, was built in 1719 and has a hammam (Turkish bath) attached – the only one of its kind in Montenegro. Ulcinj's main mosque is the **Namazgjahu Mosque**, built in 1728.

Ulcinj was once a notorious lair for pirates, who gleefully looted Venetian, Ottoman and Austrian shipping in the area – by the 15th century there were pirates from as far afield as Malta and Algeria settled at Ulcinj. Ulcinj also had a flourishing slave trade – initially, these were the owners of villas on the Dalmatian and Italian coast ransacked by the pirates, who would then ransom them for more money; later they were slaves captured in Africa. The square in front of the Church-Mosque was formerly a slave market.

There's a small beach east of the old town (Mala plaža), while Ulcinj's main beach, the larger **Velika plaža** (*velika* means 'big') is further down the coast – some 12km (7 miles) of fine golden sand, popular not just for swimming but also for kite surfing, and the location of the Southern Soul Festival (www.facebook.com/SouthernSoulFestival/) in July. Further southwest, **Ulcinj Salina** ⓱ (Ulcinj Saltpans) and **Lake Saško** are among the most important areas in Montenegro for bird life, second only to Lake Skadar. Ulcinj Saltpans are an IBA (International Bird Area) and an important stop on winter migration routes – rare species such as the little tern, stone curlew and spoonbill are just some of species you can see here, along with flamingos wading through the shallows, and sometimes Dalmatian pelican.

Montenegro's Adriatic coast comes to a full stop at **Ada Bojana** – an island in the mouth of the **River Bojana**, formed after a ship sank here in the 19th century as sediment built up around the wreck. The island is linked to the mainland by a bridge, and is now

*The fortified old town of Ulcinj*

a naturist camp. Beside the River Bojana, which flows down from Lake Skadar and forms the border with Albania, a string of restaurants serve up seafood while guests sit and watch the sunset. To enter Albania, you have to backtrack to Ulcinj and take the road north and east towards the Albanian city of Shkodër.

# ROYAL HEARTLANDS – CETINJE TO LAKE SKADAR

## HIGHLIGHTS


- Cetinje, see page 68
- Lovćen, see page 72
- Njeguši, see page 74
- Lake Skadar, see page 75


Historically, this area was the cradle of the Montenegrin state, with the capital of the medieval kingdom of Zeta being located at Žabljak Crnojevići on the northern shore of Lake Skadar in the mid-15th century, until the 1480s when its rulers were forced to relocate and found a new capital at Cetinje, abandoning the Lake Skadar area to some 400 years of Ottoman rule.

### NOTES

Montenegro also has its own, alternative version of the Creation myth. Apparently, when God was busy creating the world, he carried a large bag of stones to distribute across the earth. Except the bag broke, and the whole lot fell on Montenegro – a story which, when you look at the landscape around Cetinje (known locally as the 'sea of stone'), does seem remarkably appropriate.

## CETINJE

**Cetinje** ⓲ was founded in the 1480s by Ivan Crnojević, in the shadow of Mt Lovćen, after abandoning the lowlands of Skadarsko jezero to

*Cetinje Monastery*

the Ottomans – and it was to remain the Montenegrin capital for over four and a half centuries, until Podgorica became the capital in 1945. As well as the 15th century monastery the town has several museums and other monuments you'll want to stop and see.

The original **Cetinje Monastery** built by Ivan Crnojević in 1483 is no more – it stood in an area of town known as Ćipur, but was demolished by the Venetians in 1692. From a contemporary engraving, it appears to have been a three-nave basilica. The 'new' Cetinje Monastery (charge) was rebuilt by Danilo I in its present location – on the remains of what was once the royal palace of Ivan Crnojević – a few years later, in 1701, using stone from the original. It was subsequently torched by the Ottomans in 1714, but was again rebuilt. The monastery contains several relics, including what is said to be the hand of John the Baptist, a fragment of the true cross, and the relics of St Peter of Cetinje. It also houses a copy of *Oktoih*, the book printed by the son of Ivan Crnojević in 1494.

On the site of the original monastery at Ćipur there now stands a church (the **Church of the Birth of Our Lady**), a single-nave structure built for Prince Nikola in 1886 – which due to structural problems had to be pulled down almost immediately and rebuilt, being completed finally in 1890. Inside, there's a sarcophagus containing the remains of Ivan Crnojević and a late 19th century iconostasis, the work of craftsmen from St Petersburg. Remains of the old monastery are still visible.

There are several museums in Cetinje, which collectively form the **National Museum of Montenegro** (Narodni Muzej Crne Gore; www.narodnimuzej.me; charge).

The Historical Museum, Art Museum and Archaeology Museum are located in Vladin Dom. The **Art Museum** is divided into several collections including Montenegrin art from the late 19th to the end of the 20th century, works by artists of the former Yugoslavia, and an icon collection. One particularly valuable icon, known as the Madonna of Philermos, which occupies its own room (the 'Blue Chapel'), is linked to the Order of St John of Jerusalem (the Knights Hospitaller) who brought it from Jerusalem to the island of Rhodes, from where it later made its way

## NOTES

*Stećci* (singular *stećak*) are distinctive medieval tombstones found widely across Montenegro, Croatia and Serbia, and in particular Bosnia and Hercegovina (where there around 60,000 of them), dating mostly from the 14th–15th centuries. They were once believed to be associated with the Bogomil heresy, though this theory has since been discredited. Several *stećak* sites across all four countries gained a place on UNESCO's World Heritage List in 2016.

*The extraordinary path to Njegoš Mausoleum*

to Malta and then from 1798 St Petersburg, being brought to the Ostrog Monastery in Montenegro during the second World War.

Just to the south of Vladin Dom, the **Njegoš Museum at Biljarda** is housed within the former residence of Petar II Petrović Njegoš, built in 1838 and so named after a billiard table Njegoš had brought from Vienna, apparently the only one in Montenegro at the time. It contains a small armoury, the original manuscript of his epic poem *The Mountain Wreath*, and an enormous relief map of Montenegro from the Second World War. In the garden, there's a **Lapidarium**with several *stećak* tombstones from Montenegro.

Also part of the National Museum of Montenegro are the **Ethnographic Museum** and **King Nikola's Museum**, the latter housed within the former residence of Nikola I Petrović-Njegoš, both just to the east of Biljarda. In front of King Nikola's Museum

## FORMER EMBASSIES

Cetinje's architecture includes several former embassies, rather grand buildings which were established following the Treaty of Berlin in 1878, when players on the world stage suddenly found a need to enter diplomatic relations with Montenegro. There were eleven of them on the eve of the First World War, and with the exception of one (the United States Embassy, which was destroyed in the 1979 earthquake), all are still standing, and have found a succession of different uses.

One of the grandest is the French Embassy, which remained an embassy until 1949, since when it has housed the National Library of Montenegro. The Austro-Hungarian Embassy, which was designed by the architect Josip Slade and has a Roman Catholic chapel attached to it, today houses the Institute for the Protection of Cultural Monuments. The Russian Embassy, designed by the Italian architect Corradini in Russian baroque style, was a girls' high school between the two world wars, and since 1988 has been home to the Faculty of Fine Arts. The Italian Embassy, also designed by Corradini, is now the National Library. The British Embassy is now the Academy of Music, and the Serbian Embassy became the Ethnographic Museum in 1987.

there's a sculpture of Ivan Crnojević, made on the 500th anniversary of the founding of the city.

For a good bird's eye view of Cetinje, walk up **Orlov Krš**, the low hill on the western side of town. There's a monument on top to Danilo I Petrović-Njegoš.

## LOVĆEN

**Lovćen** ⓳ is the mountain between Kotor and Cetinje, rising steeply from the Bay of Kotor and made famous by the mausoleum of the great Montenegrin ruler Petar II Petrović-Njegoš (ruled 1830–51), which stands right on the narrow, airy summit. Described by the author J.A. Cuddon as 'probably the loneliest and windiest grave in the world', the **Njegoš Mausoleum** (charge) was built between 1970 and 1974, and consists of a small rectangular courtyard with a well at its centre, surrounded by arcades. At the far end of this, two 4.5 metre (15ft) -high caryatids in dark, polished marble frame the entrance to a crypt, which contains a statue of Petar II in black granite by the Croatian sculptor Ivan Meštrović, below a mosaic ceiling composed of some 200,000 gilded tiles. Beyond the mausoleum, a short, paved path leads to a small viewing platform which commands jaw-dropping views over the surrounding landscape. Njegoš, who was born in the nearby village of Njeguši, personally chose this as his final resting place, his remains lying in a small chapel on Lovćen until the present structure was built. It's an appropriate enough site – as well as a very able ruler, he was an accomplished poet whose *Gorski Vijenac* ('The Mountain Wreath', published in Vienna in 1847) is usually considered Montenegro's finest literary work. The tall white pole is a lightning conductor – disconcerting if you're up here at the onset of a storm.

Lovćen actually has two summits – Jezerski vrh ('lake peak', 1,657 metres/4,536ft) which is the one with the mausoleum on, referred to generically as Lovćen; and Štirovnik (1,748 metres/5,734ft), which is the higher of the two but is a restricted area closed to the public,

***Lovćen National Park***

*Njeguši, known for its ham*

since it's crowned by an enormous telecommunications tower.

Lovćen was declared **a national park** in 1952, covering an area of around 6,200 hectares (15,320 acres). The mountain slopes are heavily forested, and around 200 species of birds have been recorded within the national park including golden eagle, imperial eagle and peregrine falcon, along with some rare species of amphibian. The national park office for Lovćen is in Poda (www.nparkovi.me; charge).

There's an asphalt road from Cetinje almost to the summit of Jezerski vrh, passing the village of **Ivanova korita** where you'll find a few places to stay and eat, and the beginning of a marked footpath to the summit. At the end of the road (and footpath) is a car park and restaurant, and the beginning of a long flight of steps – 461 of them, to be precise – climbing up to the mausoleum.

## NJEGUŠI

Just west of Cetinje on the road to Kotor lies the little village of **Njeguši** ⓴, famous for its *pršut* (air-cured ham, similar to prosciutto) and as the birthplace of the Petar II Petrović-Njegoš. The house where Montenegro's great ruler-poet was born houses a modest ethnographic collection, and can be visited (charge). Beyond Njeguši, a spectacular winding road descends the mountainside to Kotor, passing the village of Krstac, from where the old 'Ladder of Cattaro' (see page 51) makes a knee-jarring descent to the city below.

## LAKE SKADAR

**Lake Skadar** (Skadarsko jezero) straddles the border between Montenegro and Albania and is the largest lake in the Balkans, surrounded by reed beds and mountains. It's a spectacularly beautifully area, its surface dotted with water lilies and water chestnuts, where local fishermen still ply the waters in traditional, flat-bottomed wooden boats, fishing for carp and bleak. Perfect for exploring by kayak, on foot or by bike, it's also one of the best birding sites in southeast Europe, and its surroundings are Montenegro's best wine producing area. If you flew into Podgorica and the

*Moored up at Virpazar*

*Grmožur's fortress*

weather was clear, you'll already have been treated to jaw-dropping aerial views of the lake as you came in to land.

One of Montenegro's five national parks, Lake Skadar is an area of huge ecological importance, with over 270 species of bird recorded here, among them the iconic but rare Dalmatian pelican, as well as pygmy cormorant (in significant numbers), grey heron, squacco heron, great crested grebe, little egret, glossy ibis and rock partridge. It is of particular importance as a stopover on winter migration routes, with up to 200,000 birds wintering here. Some areas of the lake have been designated as special reserves – Manastirska Tapija and Pančeva oka for example, which are recognised as IBAs (International Birding Areas) – and the whole lake was declared a Ramsar site (a Wetland of International Importance) in 1996. The lake also contains over 40 species of fish – among them carp, chub, grey mullet, eel and bleak – which local fishermen still catch from handmade wooden long boats called *čamac*, using fishing rods made of willow.

The surface area of Lake Skadar varies considerably between summer and winter – from an average of some 370 sq km (142 sq miles) in summer, to over 500 sq km (193 sq miles) in winter, with an average length of 44km (27 miles); its average depth is between 5 metres (16.4ft) and 8 metres (26ft). Over half of the lake lies in Montenegro, the rest in Albania. It is fed primarily by the River Morača, which flows into the lake from the north, as well as by underground karst springs, and is drained by the Bojana, which flows out of the southeast corner of the lake (in Albania) and down to the Adriatic coast near Ulcinj.

The gateway to Lake Skadar is **Virpazar** ㉑, a quiet little village on the northwest corner of the lake, near the main road between Podgorica and Bar. Virpazar is home to the **Lake Skadar National Park headquarters** (www.nparkovi.me), which is where you should head to buy your entry ticket to the national park, near the stout stone bridge. There's another national park office at Vranjina, back across the causeway on the road to Podgorica. Virpazar is just a 20-minute drive from Podgorica Airport, or if you're coming from

*Rijeka Crnojevića*

***Boating on Lake Skadar***

Cetinje there's a back road via Rijeka Crnojevića. There are regular buses from Podgorica, and you can also get here by train on the Podgorica-Bar railway line.

There's a 16th century **Ottoman fort** perched on a rocky spur just above Virpazar, which you can walk up to from the village (Tvrđava Besac; charge), and another, larger fort (Tvrđava Lessendro) on the causeway beside the main road to Podgorica. In the northwest corner of the lake itself, the rocky islet of **Grmožur** is topped with the ruins of a crumbling fortress, built by the Turks in the mid 19th century, but later in the same century used by Montenegro as a prison – something of a lonely, diminutive Alcatraz.

The vineyards to the west of Lake Skadar are some of the best in Montenegro, and **wine tours** can easily be arranged from Virpazar.

North from Virpazar heading towards Cetinje is the tiny settlement of **Rijeka Crnojevića** ㉒, where an old triple-arched stone bridge spans the River Crnojevića just before it broadens and flows into Lake Skadar. The bridge, along with the stone house next to it (now restored and turned into a fine restaurant, Konoba Mostina), was built in the 19th century by the Montenegrin ruler Danilo II Petrović. The picture-perfect view usually associated with Lake Skadar (mainly because it's the one used by the Montenegrin tourist office) is actually the River Crnojevića, rather than the lake itself, viewed from near here.

Lake Skadar sees remarkably few visitors, despite being so close to both Podgorica and the coast, with the majority of those who do come arriving on coach tours from elsewhere in the country, and staying only just long enough for a short boat trip on the lake. But it's impossible to do justice to this area in such a short visit, and it's much more rewarding to stay for two or three days, allowing enough time for kayaking or a boat tour on the lake, a food tour or a visit to local vineyards, perhaps a hike on Rumija.

*Mosaics in the Ostrog Monastery*

**Rumija** ㉓, which at 1,594 metres (5,229ft) is the highest point on the ridge of mountains southwest of the lake, makes for a great hike, either from a 4WD track high up on the mountain (part off the PPT

*Ostrog Monastery*

or Montenegrin Coastal Traverse) which if you have your own wheels you can reach from Tuđemili, or (longer) from Stari Bar. It's a short easy walk from the 4WD track, and the views from the summit are outstanding, taking in the huge expanse of Lake Skadar below, the convoluted jumble of the Prokletije peaks along the Albanian border, and clear views up the coast to Lovćen and far beyond – on a clear day, you can easily see the island of Mljet in Croatia. There's a small metal Orthodox church on the summit of Rumija, airlifted here in 2005 – rather controversially, since this was done without obtaining the requisite permit.

Despite its beauty, Lake Skadar suffers from its own environmental challenges, just like many other places in Montenegro. Rubbish and waste are washed down the River Morača into the lake, which some locals do their best to remove. There is a chronic lack of funding, and the threat of unsympathetic development never seems far away.

# DURMITOR AND THE NORTHWEST

## HIGHLIGHTS

- Northwest from Podgorica, see page 81
- Durmitor National Park, see page 82

The northwestern area of Montenegro contains its best-known mountain region, Durmitor National Park, as well as the spectacular Tara Canyon and, closer to Podgorica, Ostrog Monastery.

## NORTHWEST FROM PODGORICA

Around 20km (12.4 miles) beyond Danilovgrad on the road to Nikšić, **Ostrog Monastery** ㉔ (http://manastirostrog.com; charge) makes for a spectacular sight, it's white façade built improbably into a sheer cliff face. Built in 17th century, it is dedicated to St Basil of Ostrog (Sv Vasilije Ostroški), the former Metropolitan Bishop of Hercegovina, who is buried here. There are two cave churches, one of which houses the bones of Sv Vasilije in a reliquary, their walls decorated with 17th century frescoes by the Serbian painter Radul. The monastery was partly rebuilt in the 1920s after a fire. Ostrog is the most popular pilgrimage site in Montenegro, and it's possible to stay overnight in the monastery. From the main road it's a further 8km (5 miles) uphill to the lower and upper parts of the monastery itself.

North of Nikšić (where Montenegro's best beer, Nikšićko Pivo, is brewed) the road forks, with a road on the left going north to **Plužine**, while straight ahead leads to Šavnik and Žabljak. The main reason to head for Plužine is the Piva Canyon and **Lake Piva** (the latter created when a dam was built in the 1970s), and just before the border with Bosnia, the little settlement of **Šćepan Polje** which provides a particularly good base for white water rafting trips on the Tara and Piva rivers. To the west of Lake Piva, Bioč is a huge and very little visited mountain area extending to the Bosnian border, where trails lead over into Bosnia's Sutjeska National Park.

### NOTES

As in the Alps and other mountains, locals move their livestock up to higher pastures during the summer months, staying in small cottages which in Montenegro are called *katuni* and dot the landscape of Durmitor and other mountain areas.

*Durmitor National Park*

## DURMITOR NATIONAL PARK

Durmitor National Park (www.nparkovi.me; charge) covers an area of some 39,000 hectares (96,371 acres), approximately half of this having been classified as a UNESCO World Heritage site since 1980. A high mountain plateau between the canyons of the Tara and Piva rivers, it contains around 50 peaks higher than 2,000 metres (6,562ft) as well as numerous glacial lakes, and is incredibly rich in plants, with many species which are rare or endemic. 172 species of bird have been recorded in the park, including alpine chough, capercaillie and golden eagle. Durmitor is one of the best (and the most popular) hiking areas in Montenegro, with oodles of clearly marked trails, a couple of mountain huts and plenty of jaw-dropping views. Short walks include a circuit of Crno jezero (Black Lake), where there's a cave in which Tito took shelter during the Second World War. Longer but no less popular is the one-day hike up to Ledena pećina ('ice cave'), which – as its name implies – is filled with snow and ice throughout the year. But if you really want to see the most spectacular parts of Durmitor, a multi-day trek is far more rewarding. This can include a hike to the top of the highest mountain in Durmitor, **Bobotov kuk** (2,523 metres/8,278ft) – which is usually described as the highest peak in Montenegro, although Maja Kolata, a peak in the Prokletije mountains on the Albanian border is actually a few metres higher – and a stay at the hut on Škrčko jezero. The gateway to Durmitor is the busy little mountain town of **Žabljak** ㉕, situated at an altitude of around 1,450 metres (4,757ft).

Cutting across the northeast side of the national park, the emerald-green of the River Tara rushes through the **Tara Canyon** – the deepest canyon in Europe, reaching a depth of 1,300 metres (4,265ft) and the second deepest in the world after the Grand Canyon – which is extremely popular for white water rafting. For the best view of the canyon at its deepest point, you can easily walk (or hire mountain bikes) from Žabljak to a spectacular viewpoint on the edge of the canyon at Ćurevac (8km (5 miles) on roads followed by a fairly easy 30-minute walk along a path at the end).

It's possible to get from Žabljak to Plužine without backtracking to Šavnik, by following a (fairly rough) road through Trsa – an area of highland pastures reputed to make the best *kaymak* (similar to clotted cream) in Montenegro.

## NOTES

In May 1943 a small party of British officers, including F.W.D. Deakin, parachuted into highland Montenegro, landing on Durmitor, as the first British military mission to Tito. Later that year Deakin was succeeded by Fitzroy Maclean. Both Deakin and Maclean wrote books based on their experiences behind enemy lines in the Balkans (Deakin's *The Embattled Mountain* was published in 1971, Maclean's *Eastern Approaches* in 1949).

# THE NORTHEAST

## HIGHLIGHTS


- East from Žabljak, see page 85
- Biogradska Gora National Park, see page 86
- Plav and Prokletije, see page 88


With just a couple of exceptions, Montenegro's mountainous and rural northeast is the least visited part of the country. While Biogradska Gora National Park, the Morača Monastery and (in winter) the ski resort on Bjelasica do see a stream of visitors (though in much, much smaller numbers than anywhere on the coast) the same cannot be said for much else in the region – despite being home to

*Tara Bridge, a one-time record holder*

the country's newest national park (Prokletije), one of the largest glacial lakes in the region (Lake Plav), outstanding hiking and biking trails and some of the most sublimely beautiful mountain scenery in Europe.

*Biogradska Gora National Park*

## EAST FROM ŽABLJAK

From Durmitor and Žabljak, it's possible to reach the northeast corner of Montenegro without backtracking to Podgorica (though if you're travelling by bus, that is indeed what you'll have to do) providing you either have a car (or a bike), or are taking a taxi. The old road east to Mojkovac follows the Tara, through some beautiful scenery and passing tall stands of black pine, but is steep in places and has many hairpin bends.

Soon after meeting the Tara there's a junction, with a road heading north towards Pljevlje (where you'll find the 16th century Hussein Pasha Mosque), over the **Tara Bridge** (Đurđevića Tara). At well over 150 metres (492ft) high and 365 metres (1,197ft) long, this was the largest concrete arched bridge in Europe at the time it was built in 1940. The bridge has five arches, one of which was detonated during the Second World War by the Partisans – with the help of one of the bridge's engineers, Lazar Jauković – to prevent the advance of Italian troops. This successfully cut the only crossing point of the Tara Canyon, without destroying the bridge entirely, but meant that Jauković had to remain on the wrong side, and was captured and executed by the Italians for his efforts. The damaged part of the bridge was reconstructed in 1946.

Continue east from the Tara Bridge to reach the small town of **Mojkovac**, where the road splits again – south to Biogradska Gora National Park, Kolašin and Podgorica, north and then east to Bijelo Polje, Plav and Prokletije.

## BIOGRADSKA GORA NATIONAL PARK

**Biogradska Gora National Park** (www.nparkovi.me; charge) lies just south of Mojkovac – an area of remarkably intact, undisturbed forest. The area was declared a national park in 1952, having already been under special protection since 1878, by order of Nikola I Petrovic-Njegoš. The national park covers an area of 5,650 hectares (13,961 acres), at the heart of which is Biogradsko jezero (Lake Biogradska), the surrounding hills cloaked in dense forest, giving way to more rounded summits and rolling grasslands, quite a contrast to the wildly jagged profile of surrounding mountain ranges. Some 2000 plant species have been identified within the national park (including 90 species of tree), 20 percent of them endemic to the Balkan peninsula. You'll find the entrance to the park, and the national park office where you can buy your entry ticket, on the shore of Biogradsko jezero, along a 4WD road which leads off the main road around 7km (4.3 miles) south of Mojkovac. A walk around Biogradsko jezero makes for an easy and very pleasant 1-hour hike, some of it on broad forest paths, some on wooden boardwalks.

### NOTES

The Raška Style (so named after the medieval Serbian state of Raška) represents the apogee of ecclesiastical art in medieval Serbia. Among the best examples of the style are the frescoes at Studnica, Đurđevi stupovi and Sopoćani monasteries in Serbia, and the Morača Monastery in Montenegro.

*A local mosque in the area around Plav*

To the east of Biogradska Gora, and part of the same group of gently rounded mountains, is **Bjelasica**, home during the winter to Montenegro's only well-developed **ski resort**, Kolašin 1450 (access from Kolašin, http://kolasin1450.com). Access is from the small mountain town of **Kolašin** ㉖.

After around 15km (9 miles) the road south from Kolašin passes the **Morača Monastery** ㉗ (charge), founded in the 13th century by the Serbian prince Stefan Vukanović Nemanjić, nephew of King Stefan the First-Crowned, the first king of medieval Serbia. It's a remarkable building, with some exceptional frescoes dating from the 13th or 14th century, as well as later frescoes from the 16th and 17th centuries. The earlier frescoes depict scenes from the life of St Elijah (Sv Ilija), and are outstanding examples of the so-called Raška Style.

East from Kolašin, a fairly rough road leads over a pass near the Komovi peaks and down to Andrijevica, providing a convenient shortcut to Plav and Prokletije National Park. South from Kolašin, the main road follows the River Morača to Podgorica, while the Belgrade-Bar railway line threads its way across the hillsides on the opposite side of the river.

## PLAV AND PROKLETIJE

East from Mojkovac, the road leads to Berane and on to Rožaje in the far eastern corner of Montenegro. Beyond Rožaje, a spectacular road winds up to the Čakor Pass on the border with Kosovo, a route only suitable for 4X4 vehicles and daring drivers. Turning south from Berane, the road follows the River Lim to **Lake Plav** (Plavsko jezero), a beautiful glacial lake at an altitude of around 900 metres (2,953ft), below Mt Visitor and on the edge of the Prokletije mountains. Lake Plav is fed from the southwest by the River Ljuča, and drained at its northern end by the **River Lim**, a major tributary of the River Drina which it meets around 200km (124 miles) later in Bosnia. The glacier (long since vanished) which formed this area is thought to have been one of the largest in the Balkans.

There's an excellent place to stay on the shore of the lake (Kula Damjanova), and the little town of **Plav** ㉘ is where you'll find the office and information centre for Prokletije National Park – one of the few places in Montenegro where you can get detailed, accurate information on hiking

### NOTES

It's possible to cycle around the lake – a circuit from Plav to Gusinje along the western shore, returning along the eastern shore, is around 30km (18.6 miles), and the route is fairly flat and all on asphalt, with very little traffic. Around halfway between Plav and Gusinje, a minor (partly unsurfaced) road leads over the Ljuča, turning the circuit into a figure of eight.

*Hiking in the stunning landscape of the Prokletije Mountains*

or mountain biking in this area. Fly-fishing is popular in the area around Lake Plav, and it's a magnificent area for hiking and cycling. The outstanding trans-border hiking route, the Peaks of the Balkans Trail, goes through Plav (see page 91).

Lake Plav is not the only lake in the area worth seeing, though it's certainly the most accessible. **Hridsko jezero**, east of Plav and only about 2km (1.2 miles) short of the Albanian border, sits in a spectacular setting below the Bogićevica peaks, at an altitude of around 2,000 metres (6,562ft). Several hiking trails set off towards it from Plav, though on foot it would make for a very long day from Plav (around 14km/8.7 miles each way), so it's more feasible as a mountain bike route, or you can even drive part of the way. **Visitorsko jezero**, to the west of Plav, lies on the northern slopes of Mt Visitor and can be reached by a decent 4WD road.

Southwest of Plav at the entrance to the Grbaja and Ropojana valleys lies the hardly little village of **Gusinje**, which along with Plav provides a gateway to **Prokletije National Park** (www.nparkovi.me; charge) – Montenegro's fifth and newest – which was designated a national park in 2009, and covers an area of 16,630 hectares (41,093 acres). This area has a large Albanian population, and you'll see small mosques with distinctive wooden minarets. When the intrepid British traveller Edith Durham travelled through the Prokletije mountains in the early years of the 20th century, she described Gusinje as 'the Lhasa of Europe' thanks to how remote and hard to access it was at the time (though in fairness, the difficulty in a getting to this area was more one of politics than geography).

*Grbaja Valley in Prokletije National Park*

## TRANS-BORDER TRAILS

The **Peaks of the Balkans Trail** is an epic trans-border route through the mountains in Montenegro, Albania and Kosovo – visiting remote valleys and mountain passes, surrounded by the towering peaks of the Prokletije mountains (which translate as 'the accursed mountains'), with traditional village homestays offering food and accommodation. The route is 192km (119 miles) -long and can be done in around 10 days; there is a detailed map available of the whole route as well as a good website to peruse with route descriptions (www.peaksofthebalkans.com).

The mountains of Montenegro also lie on another new trans-border route, the **Via Dinarica** (http://viadinarica.com), which stretches some 2,000km (1,243ft) along the spine of the Dinaric Alps, through some of the least-known mountains in Europe – from Slovenia in the north, through Croatia, Bosnia, Montenegro (entering the country from Bosnia's Sutjeska National Park, exiting in Prokletije), Albania, Kosovo and Macedonia. The Via Dinarica is still under development and there are several variants to the route, rather than one single trail – a 'cultural corridor', as it has been described.

It's a further 7km (4.3 miles) or so from Gusinje to the head of the **Grbaja Valley**, where the road peters out and hiking trails shoot up the surrounding mountains, watched over by spiky peaks with names like Očnjak (meaning 'fang'), Karanfili ('carnations') and Kolje ('spear'). The most straightforward hike in the valley is up to the summit of Volušnica – though be aware that even though the walking on this route is perfectly easy, there's a whopping great drop on the eastern side of Volušnica, almost all the way to the valley floor. The views across the valley however, to the sheer-sided Karanfili peaks, are sensational. Just to the southeast of Gusinje itself, Ali Paša Spring (a natural pool fed by springs) makes for a nice easy walk. Further south from Gusinje, another long glacial valley, the Ropojana, was a former trade route – and is now where the Peaks of the Balkans Trail disappears over the border into Albania.

*Hiking in Durmitor National Park*

# Things to do

## OUTDOOR ACTIVITIES

Montenegro is a truly outstanding destination for outdoor, active and adventure holidays, with some incredible hiking on offer along some of the least frequented trails in Europe, along with mountain biking, kayaking, white water rafting and more, plus some excellent spots for bird watching. Skiing is also possible, though as yet it remains rather underdeveloped.

### HIKING

Montenegro is one of the best, and least known hiking destinations in Europe – a landscape literally bristling with mountain peaks and slashed by stupendously deep canyons, with an extensive network of well-marked hiking trails (and very few people on them).

There are five national parks, and detailed local hiking maps, and access to most of the main hiking areas is easy, even with public transport. There are a few mountain huts in Montenegro, but not many, so any serious multi-day hiking trip usually means carrying a tent. Trails are marked using red-and-white trail markings.

On balance, the best hiking destination in Montenegro is Durmitor, which has some great one-day as well as multi-day hikes. Even more spectacular and much less visited is Prokletije, with some magnificent walks in the Grbaja Valley. Rumija, between Lake Skadar and Stari Bar, makes for a great day hike (there's a trail starting beside the old town in Stari Bar, while a walk around Biogradsko jezero in Biogradsko Gora National Park makes a very easy lakeside walk which can be completed in one hour, surrounded by unspoiled forest.

Montenegro has two well-established long-distance trails, the **Primorska Planinarska Transverzala** and **Crnogorska Transversala**, and there are also some truly epic trans-border routes, the excellent **Peaks of the Balkans Trail** (www.peaksofthebalkans.

com, see page 91) and the **Via Dinarica** (http://viadinarica.com). It is safe to say both of these have been 'discovered' in recent years due to bloggers and vloggers hitting the paths, but you'll still find these routes wonderfully low-key with genuinely hospitable places to stay and an often 'off the map' feel to things.

The 182km- (113 mile-) **Montenegrin Coastal Traverse** (Primorska Planinarska Transverzala or PPT) starts on the coast at Herceg Novi in the north, climbing to Subra and Orjen before continuing above the

## HIKING RESOURCES

**Maps**

Durmitor and Tara Canyon – Durmitor National Park (1:25,000; Geokarta)

Hiking and Biking Tourist Map, Montenegro – NP Durmitor (1:50,000; COSv/US Aid)

Bjelasica and Komovi Mountain Tourist Map (1:50,000; Huber Verlag/GIZ)

Skadar Lake National Park (1:55,000; Lake Skadar NP/Austrian development Cooperation/GTZ/Huber)

Prokletije Hiking and Biking (1:50,000; Huber Verlag/GIZ)

Peaks of the Balkans (1:60,000; Huber Verlag/GIZ)

**Hiking guidebooks**

Rudolf Abraham *The Mountains of Montenegro* (Cicerone)

Rudolf Abraham *Peaks of the Balkans Trail* (Cicerone)

**Local tour operators**

Black Mountain (www.montenegroholiday.com) *Covering all of Montenegro, including the Peaks of the Balkans Trail*

Adria Trek (tel: 069 678 952) *Montenegro*

Undiscovered Montenegro (www.undiscoveredmontenegro.com) *Lake Skadar area*

Green Visions (tel: (Bosnia) +387 (0)33 717 290; www.greenvisions.ba) *Bosnia*

Outdoor Albania (www.outdooralbania.com) *Albania*

**Mountaineering Association of Montenegro**

Planinarski Savez Crne Gore (www.pscg.me)

*Biking a mountain road near Kotor Bay*

Bay of Kotor to Lovćen, then through Pastrovska gora to Rumija, and down to the coast again at Stari Bar in the south. The total distance is 182km (113 miles), but unless you're carrying food for the whole route and wild camping (not possible in Lovćen National Park anyway), you need to add getting to and from accommodation, food and supplies – of which there's virtually none on the route itself. Many sections of the PPT are on 4WD tracks rather than paths, and the route is mostly well signposted. Several tour operators cover this route or sections of it, including **Black Mountain** (see box, page 94) and **Undiscovered Montenegro** (see box, page 13).

The **Montenegrin Traverse** (Crnogorska Transversala or CT-1) is an altogether longer and more demanding route, stretching from the Kučka krajina mountains near the Albanian border, north through the Komovi mountains, across Bjelasica, Biogradska Gora National Park

***Durmitor National Park***

and Sinjajevina, finishing in Durmitor National Park in the north of the country. Many sections of the CT-1 are very remote, and route finding potentially more difficult. The length of the CT-1 is 164km (102 miles), and again, there are comparatively few opportunities for buying food along the way, and you need to camp on some (though not all) stages.

## MOUNTAIN BIKING

There are plenty of places in Montenegro offering some great mountain biking, both inland as well as on the coast, and in the last two decades a good network of marked cycling trails has been developed across much of the country.

A good series of booklets covering cycling routes by region have been published, with route descriptions, maps and route profiles, and these can be picked up (for free) at local tourist offices and national park offices, or downloaded from tourist office websites. The best specialist guidebook to get hold of is *Montenegro Wilderness Biking Atlas* (Map Solutions). This traces 17 mountain bike routes in Montenegro, and includes route maps at a scale of 1:100,000.

Bike trails are marked with yellow signs, and 'cycle-friendly' accommodation has been brought together under a Bed and Bike scheme.

Main roads are less suitable for cycling, the main coastal highway in particular, which sees an enormous volume of traffic in the summer, while road users tend to drive alarmingly fast. Stick to 4WD tracks and back roads instead, it's more rewarding and safer.

## KAYAKING

Without any doubt, the best destination for kayaking in Montenegro is Lake Skadar, a vast watery wilderness where comparisons with China's Guilin do not seem too far off the mark. **Undiscovered Montenegro** (see box, page 13) offer kayak holidays on Lake Skadar in April, May, June, September and October with a BCU qualified kayak coach, with kayak hire and all safety equipment included. Packages include accommodation, a welcome dinner and guided kayaking tours.

*Kayaking on Lake Skadar*

## RAFTING

Rafting on the River Tara – through the deepest canyon

in Europe, part of Durmitor National Park and a UNESCO World Heritage Site as well as a UNESCO Biosphere Reserve – is one of the most well-established outdoor sports in Montenegro. There's also rafting on the River Piva and over the border in Bosnia.

The rafting season on the Tara typically runs from mid April to the end of September. April, May and June have the highest volume of water, so are suitable for the more adventurous; July, August and September see water levels drop, and are therefore more suitable for families with young children.

There are numerous local outfits offering rafting trips, both one-day outings and multi-day trips, the latter staying at rafting camps and bungalows on the Tara or Piva.

**Rafting Montenegro** (tel: 069 310 848; www.raftingmontenegro.com) are based in Šćepan Polje (just 5km (3 miles) before the Bosnian border), where they operate from the well-equipped Waterfall Rafting Centre on the River Piva. They offer several packages, including a three-day rafting trip along the entire navigable part of the Tara, from Šljivansko to Šćepan Polje (around 90km/56 miles, approximately 10 hours rafting) and a one-day rafting trip from Šćepan Polje (18km/11 miles, 4 hours rafting).

**Black Mountain** (see box, page 94) also offer rafting trips on the Tara.

*Rafting in Tara National Park*

*Kite surfing*

It may sound obvious, but rafting, by definition, involves getting very wet. Wetsuits are supplied on rafting trips, and dry-seal bags, but it's a good policy to take as little with you as possible – if you wear glasses, some sort of safety strap for them is a good idea.

## KITE SURFING

Velika plaža, the long sandy beach south of Ulcinj, is a particularly good spot for kite surfing. **Kite Loop** (www.kiteloop.net) run a kite surfing school there and have equipment for hire.

## SKIING

Skiing in Montenegro is in its infancy, although its potential – loads of high mountains, and guaranteed snow for several months of the winter – is certainly very good.

*Perfect conditions for skiing*

The best skiing area in Montenegro – in fact the only area developed for the sport thus far – is Bjelasica, near the small mountain town of Kolašin. Winter action is centred on **Kolašin 1450** (www.kolasin1450.com), a good, fully functional ski resort with around 16.5km (10 miles) of groomed slopes and trails, new or modernised ski lifts, ski hire, a ski school with qualified instructors, a restaurant and café, a first aid centre and other facilities such as accommodation options. All this comes with fewer crowds than better-known ski resorts in the Alps, and at a fraction of the cost, though real snow cover is erratic to say the least.

Kolašin 1450 sits at an altitude of – you guessed it – 1,450 metres (4757ft), with around 40 percent of its runs being graded 'easy', while there are steeper and more challenging runs higher up (the highest run starts from an altitude of 1,973m/6,473ft), and there's a Nordic circuit, as well as plenty of scope to go off-piste. Ski lifts are open 9.30am–4pm and the best conditions for skiing are between mid December and mid February. It's a 15-minute drive between the resort and the little mountain town of Kolašin.

**Explorer** (www.explorer.co.me) are a Kolašin-based agency, offering a wide range winter activities, including all-inclusive 3- or 7-day ski packages on Bjelasica, with 4-star accommodation, half board, ski passes and ski hire.

## BIRD WATCHING

A Ramsar site, a national park and home to two IBAs (International Birding Areas), Lake Skadar is one of the best birding sites in Europe, with over 270 species of bird having been recorded here, many of them quite rare – including the iconic Dalmatian pelican, squacco heron, rock partridge, little egret, and a huge colony of pygmy cormorants – with up to 200,000 birds wintering here on their migration routes. The best time to visit Lake Skadar is in May, if bird watching is your primary reason for coming. You need to get out on the lake itself to have a chance of getting within reasonably good sighting distance of the pelicans, which means going out on a boat with a knowledgeable local guide (and one who is sensitive to not getting too close to the birds or scaring them).

*Dalmatian pelican, Skadar Lake*

*Traditional Montenegrin hand-painted decorative plates and vases*

**Undiscovered Montenegro** (see box, page 13) are the best people to contact about arranging a birding tour on Lake Skadar. They offer group bird watching holidays with an expert guide (Andrej Vizi, who is Curator of the National History Museum of Montenegro and the authority behind the monitoring of winter birds nationwide), including guided excursions.

**Boat Milica** (http://boatmilica.com) are also a good, knowledgeable local outfit running general and birding tours on the lake.

Other places in Montenegro good for birding include the Ulcinj salt pans (another IBA), particularly during migration, and Durmitor National Park. **Darko Saveljić** is a local ornithologist and bird guide specialising in the Ulcinj Saltpans (email: dasav@t-com.me); **Marko Raković** is an ornithologist and bird guide specialising in Durmitor and the Tara Canyon (email: markorakovic@gmail.com).

# SHOPPING

Souvenirs to bring back from Montenegro include local wine and olive oil, Njeguši ham and cheese, natural soap made from olive oil, locally made jewellery and handicrafts. Although there are shops at Podgorica airport they tend to be slightly overpriced, and rather than rely on those you'd do better to shop for souvenirs during your trip – at markets, vineyards and festivals.

## WINE

If you want to buy a bottle or two of Montenegrin wine to take home with you, a good place to shop for it is the **Plantaže** vineyard shop/cellar on the Podgorica-Bar road beside Lake Skadar, near Virpazar (www.plantaze.com). A barrique-aged Vranac – made from Montenegro's signature grape – is usually the best to go for. You can also buy bottles at many of the smaller wineries, including the Klisić and Buk wineries, both of them a little west of Virpazar, and each producing a good barrique-aged Vranac.

*An old olive tree*

## RAKIJA

Rakija is available from many of the country's vineyards, often in attractive bottles which make nice souvenirs and gifts to take home.

## FOOD

*Pršut* from Njeguš and local cheeses are widely available

*Rakija*

on markets and in supermarkets, though you might need to check customs regulations on bringing meat and dairy produce back home from outside the EU or your home country.

## OLIVE OIL

Montenegro produces some very good olive oils, especially in the Bar area. One of them, called 42°N 19°E, is a limited edition olive oil made exclusively from the yields of ancient trees (some more than 2000 years old) in the Stari Bar area.

A good opportunity to taste, and buy, local olive oils is at the annual Maslinijada (Olive Tree Festival), held in Stari Bar in early November. The **Olive Oil Association of Montenegro** also have a list of olive oil producers in the Bar/Ulcinj area at (http://oliveoilmontenegro.me).

## NATURAL SOAPS

Ulcinj-based Ela Magic produces handmade natural soaps, made from a blend of olive oil, herbs, goats' milk, honey and essential oils (http://oliveoilmontenegro.me/portfolio-item/elamagic).

## HANDICRAFTS

You can sometimes buy small religious paintings and icons at some of the larger monasteries. Wood from olive trees that no longer produce yields is also used to create hand carved objects.

# ENTERTAINMENT

## FILM

Montenegro's biggest film festival is held in Herceg Novi in August (see page 40).

## THEATRE

The main theatre festival in Montenegro is **City of Theatre** (http://gradteatar.me), a long-running international theatre festival which takes place in Budva between mid June and mid August, against a backdrop of the walls of the ancient old town. There's also a **Festival of Children's Theatre** (www.kotorart.me) in Kotor in June.

*Revellers at Sea Dance Festival*

## MUSIC

There are several big international music festivals on the Montenegrin coast: **Sea Dance Festival** (www.seadancefestival.me) takes place on Budva's Jaz Beach in July; **Southern Soul Festival** (www.southernsoulfestival.me), an international soul and dance music festival, takes place on Velika Plaža Beach in Ulcinj, also in July; and **Sea Rock Festival** (http://searock.me), a rock music festival with major international acts, takes place in Kotor in June. For something altogether more chilled out, there's the **Petrovac Jazz Festival** in September; and in May there's an **International Accordion Festival** (www.harmonikafest.me) in Tivat.

## NIGHTLIFE

The place with the greatest concentration of clubs and bars in Montenegro is Budva, with one club seeming to merge into another along Slovenska Beach and some of the bigger establishments staying open to 5am, while others close at a more modest 1am or 2am. **Top Hill** (www.tophill.me), on a hill above the town, is the largest open-air club in Montenegro, with a capacity of over 5,000; clubs on Slovenska Beach include **Trocadero** and **Maltez**. For something smaller (though no less busy) head for one of the places in or around the old town, such as **Casper**, **El Mundo** or **Greco**. Alternatively, if you're in Kotor, there's **Maxiclub** (www.maxiclub.me). Podgorica also has several clubs, including **Mint Club** (one of the largest) and **Velvet** (one of the more upmarket), and plenty of bars which often have live music and DJs into the early hours of the morning – **Nice Vice**, **Soul II Soul** and **Buda Bar** to name just a few.

### NOTES

Parents with young kids should take note that there's a soft play area within Budva's main bus station. Kids' playgrounds in Podgorica can be found at Timberland Djeciji Park (in Njegošev Park) and in Tološi Park.

*Budva Carnival*

## ACTIVITIES FOR CHILDREN

Children will be welcomed in Montenegro with typical Mediterranean warmth. Montenegro's greatest draw cards for children are its beaches (those at Bečići, Pržno near Sv Stefan and another Pržno near Tivat are good for kids) and the great outdoors – take them out on a boat or kayak on Lake Skadar, armed with a pair of binoculars for spotting some of its amazing birdlife; walk with them around Biogradsko Lake; hire mountain bikes or take them for a short – or long – hike in Durmitor.

## FESTIVALS AND EVENTS

**January:** *Orthodox Christmas*, 6th January (Christmas Eve)–8th January; *Orthodox New Year*, 14th January.

**February:** *Carnival*, February/March – traditional (masked) processions in several towns (Kotor, Prčnj etc) on the last Sunday before Lent; *Mimosa Festival*, Herceg Novi –various cultural events, music and processions.

**March/April:** *Easter*, March/April.

**May:** *Harmonika Fest (International Accordion Festival),* Tivat – festival of traditional accordion playing (www.harmonikafest.me); Budva Carnival - Rio-style carnival with participation from across the Balkans and Italy.

**June:** *Sea Rock Festival*, Kotor – rock music festival with major international acts (http://searock.me); *KotorArt Festival*, Kotor/Perast, June/July – several festivals rolled into one, including an International Festival of Klapa in Perast, and a Children's Theatre Festival in Kotor (www.kotorart.me).

**July:** *Southern Soul Festival*, Velika Plaža Beach, Ulcinj – international soul and dance music festival (www.southernsoulfestival.me); *Fašinada*, Perast, 22 July –procession of colourful boats around the tiny island of Gospa od Škrplja at dusk; *Sea Dance Festival*, Jaz Beach, Budva (www.seadancefestival.me); *Budva City of Theatre Festival*, Budva, mid June–mid August – long-running international theatre festival (http://gradteatar.me).

**August:** *Herceg Novi Film Festival*, Herceg Novi, first week of August (www.filmfestival.me); *Boka Nights*, Kotor, third Saturday in August – illuminated flotilla of boats, fireworks and other festivities; *Petrovac Night*, Petrovac – large traditional festival, with plenty of wine and grilled fish.

**September:** *Petrovac Jazz Festival*, Petrovac – international and local jazz artists.

**October:** *Days of Širun*, Budva – traditional fisherman's festival

**November:** *Maslinijada (Olive Tree Festival*), Stari Bar – festival of olive oil and olive growers (http://oliveoilmontenegro.me); Podgorica Marathon/half marathon (www.podgorica.run)

**December:** *Festival of Wine and Bleak*, Virpazar – celebration of food and wine from the Lake Skadar region.

# Food and drink

Montenegro lies at the crossroads of several different culinary influences – Mediterranean and Italian on the coast, with the legacy of several centuries of Ottoman Turkish rule inland, and hints of the cuisine of neighbouring Albania in the south. Meat dishes feature prominently in Montenegrin cuisine – usually veal or lamb, although away from the coast you may also find wild boar and other game on the menu, while you'll see both freshwater fish offered inland and seafood on the coast. The wine is surprisingly good (and cheap), the best coming from the area west of Lake Skadar. Vegetarian and vegan dishes aren't the speciality, but you'll usually always find something tasty on the menu to satisfy.

*Street cafes by the seaport in Porto Montenegro*

# TOP 10 THINGS TO TRY

## 1. FISH

Along the Adriatic coast, fish is always a big part of any menu, as it is in neighbouring Croatia and Albania. Fish is usually prepared simply – grilled or fried, and served with a drizzle of pungent local olive oil. The traditional accompaniments are boiled potatoes (krompir) and Swiss chard (blitva).

## 2. SEAFOOD

The king of the restaurant table, summertime seafood dinners are a memorable Montenegro experience. Grilled squid (*lignje*), mussels (*mušulje*), and octopus salad (*salata od hobotnice*) are the occupants of the deep that find their way onto plates most commonly.

*Fish stew*

## 3. SOUP

It may not be the first thing that comes to mind when someone mentions Montenegrin food, but soups play a big part in everyday eating habits. Look out for fish soup (*riblja čorba*), veal soup (*teleći čorba*) and nettle soup (*čorba od kopriva*).

## 4. PRŠUT

The most typical appetiser served in Montenegro is *pršut* – local dry-cured ham

*A cured meat and cheese selection*

(similar to Italian prosciutto), most famously coming from the village of Njeguši, between Kotor and Cetinje on the slopes of Mt Lovćen.

## 5. GRILLED MEAT

Meat dishes feature heavily on local menus. *Ćevapčići* are small, elongated grilled meatballs, usually served with *ajvar* – onion, chips and bread while, *ražnjići* are grilled pieces of meat on skewers. *Pljeskavica* is a huge, minced meat pattie served in sauce. Njeguški steak is pork fillet stuffed with *pršut* and cheese, *popeci* are small mince fritters, also stuffed with *pršut* and cheese.

## 6. MEAT ISPOD SAČ

A distinctive and absolutely delicious way of preparing lamb, veal and other meat is, cooked in a pan under an iron bowl over (and

## NOTES

This is an excellent local initiative, which showcases the delicious cuisine of the Lake Skadar region. As well as listing good local restaurants, and their opening times, it includes a 108-page book of mouth-watering recipes, complete with English translation, which you can download for free as a pdf (http://ethnogastro-balkan.net).

scattered with) hot coals. Must be ordered a day in advance at restaurants.

## 7. BUREK

*Common across the Balkans, this* is a delicious, filled pastry, either with cheese *(sa sirom)* or with meat *(sa mesom)*, or less commonly with spinach *(sa spanaćem)*. Great for a filling picnic on the beach or in the mountains.

## 8. FRUIT

There is an abundance of fresh, seasonal fruit in Montenegro – grapes (grožđe), quince (dunja), figs (smokve), pomegranate (šipka), plums (šljive) and blueberries (borovnice).

## 9. POLENTA

*Kačamak* is a potato, cornmeal and cheese dish while *cicvara* is a mixture of cornmeal, cheese and cream.

## 10. FRESHWATER FISH

Lake Skadar provides an abundant source of carp (*krap*), bleak (*ukljeva*) and eel (*jegulja*), best enjoyed as fresh as possible at lakeside restaurants. Trout are found in most of the country's rivers.

# WHERE TO EAT

There are two main types of eatery in Montenegro, the *restoran* (restaurant) and the *konoba* (tavern). A *konoba* will usually be cheaper than a *restoran*, and less formal – however that in no way means the quality of food or service will be inferior, indeed some of the country's top places to eat are in fact called a *konoba*. In addition, quick snacks and coffee and cakes can be had at various kinds of café.

## WHEN TO EAT

Breakfast (doručak) in large hotels will usually be of the familiar continental variety – a wide spread of cereals, bread and pastries, cured meats and cheeses, eggs, sausage and other cooked meat, coffee, tea and juice. Montenegrins themselves are likely to have something simpler – bread, cheese, ham, fruit, and of course coffee. Lunch (ručak) is the main meal of the day for Montenegrins, dinner (večera) a lighter affair (though that doesn't mean it needs to be that way round for you – you can just as easily find the same food available in the afternoon as in the evening).

*A choice of Montenegrin alcohol*

*A sunny lakeside cafe*

# WHAT TO DRINK

## WINE

Crmnica, the area to the northwest of Lake Skadar, is the best wine-producing area in the country. Montenegro's signature grape variety is Vranac, producing a great big full-bodied mouthful of a red, at its best when it's been aged a couple of years to round it out a bit, but also drunk younger, when its colour is a little lighter, with a nose full of berries. As in neighbouring countries red wine is called *crno vino*, literally 'black wine'. Other local grape varieties include Krstač, which is used to produce a dry white.

## VINEYARDS TO VISIT NEAR LAKE SKADAR

Plantaže vineyard, the largest in the country, has a cellar and shop at the entrance to Lake Skadar National Park, near Virpazar. There are also many small vinyards in the villages just west of Virpazar. Among theses are the award-winning Klisić winery, in the village of Limlijani, where owner Ilija Klisić makes a lovely barrique-aged Vranac (not to mention a nice dry Muscat, among other wines), and the (also award-winning) Buk winery, highlights of which include another oak-aged Vranac and an un-oaked Chardonnay (the highest produced Chardonnay in Montenegro).

## RAKIJA

If you fancy something a little stronger than wine, there's *rakija* – an extremely potent spirit, made with grapes, plums or other fruit, or with walnuts. In Montenegro, everyone has an uncle or a grandfather or a cousin or at least knows *someone* who makes their own *rakija*, and it's highly unlikely that you'll leave the country without sampling a good *domaći* ('homemade') at some point.

## COFFEE

The ritual of drinking coffee and watching the world go by, quite possibly discussing local politics, is as much of a way of life in Montenegro as it is elsewhere around the Adriatic. As well as espresso, you'll also find Turkish coffee inland and near the Albanian border.

# MENU READER

**ajvar** roasted red pepper relish
**bijelo vino** white wine
**blitva** swiss chard
**borovnice** blueberries
**brancin** sea bass
**burek** cheese- or meat-filled pastry
**čaj** tea
**ćevapčići** (sometimes just written **ćevapi**) small grilled meatballs
**čorba** or **supa** soup
**crno vino** red wine
**dimljena** smoked
**divlja svinja** wild boar
**dunja** quince
**gambori** prawns
**gljive** mushrooms
**grdoba** monkfish
**grožđe** grapes
**gulaš** goulash
**hleb** bread
**hobotnica** octopus
**jagnjetina** lamb
**jaje** eggs
**japraci** stuffed vine leaves
**jastog** lobster
**jegulja** eel
**kafa** coffee
**kajmak** similar to clotted cream
**karpaćo** carpaccio
**kobasica** sausage

**kolač** cake
**krap** carp
**krastovac** cucumber
**krompir** potatoes
**kupus** cabbage
**lignje** squid
**maslinke** olives
**meso** meat
**mljeko** milk
**mušulje** mussels
**na žaru** grilled
**orada** gilthead bream
**palačinke** pancakes
**palamida** bonito
**paradajz** tomato
**pastrmka** trout
**patlidžan** aubergine
**piletina** chicken
**pita** filled pastry
**pivo** beer
**pljeskavica** minced meat pattie
**pomfrit** french fries
**povrće** vegetables
**pršut** prosciutto
**punjene paprike** stuffed peppers
**raštan** collard greens
**ražnjići** grilled pieces of meat on skewers
**riba** fish
**riblja čorba** fish soup
**riž** rice
**rižot** risotto
**roštilj** grill, bbq
**salata** salad
**šampinjon** mushrooms (white)
**sanpjer** John Dory
**sarma** cabbage leaves stuffed with rice and meat
**sipa** cuttlefish
**sir** cheese
**skorup** skimmed cream
**skuša** or **lokarda** mackerel
**sladoled** ice cream
**šipka** pomegranate
**školjke** shellfish
**šljive** plums
**smokve** figs
**šopska salata** cucumber, tomato, onions and sheep's cheese salad
**srdele** sardines
**stek** steak
**šunka** ham
**svinjatina** pork
**svinjski file** pork fillet
**teleća čorba** veal soup
**teleći kotlet** veal cutlet
**teletina** veal
**ukljeva** bleak
**umak** sauce
**vino** wine
**voda** water
**vrganje** porcini mushrooms

# Places to eat

Price categories reflect the cost of a two-course meal per person.
**€€€** = €25 and above
**€€** = €15–€25
**€** = under €15

## PODGORICA

**Crnogorska Kuća** Dalmatinska ulica 130b; tel: 069 300 501. 2km (1.2 miles) northwest from the city centre. Traditional Montenegrin dishes including marinated and smoked carp, grilled trout, lamb cooked in milk, *kačamak*, *kastradina* with cabbage, in a rustic stone and wood interior with red and white tablecloths and a few ancient pistols on the walls. Accommodation is also offered (2 singles, 4 doubles). **€€**

**Kalabrija** Ivana Crnojevica 59; tel: 020 634 899. Small place with an attractive, light-flooded interior, small wooden tables and a mish-mash of bric-a-brac. Widely tipped as serving the best pizzas in town. **€€**

**Lanterna** Marka Miljanova 41; www.laterna.me. Popular place with Italian and other dishes in a rustic interior – pizzas, grills, salads. Hard to escape the cigarette smoke though. **€€**

**Pod Volat** Trg Vojvode Bećir Bega Osmanagića; tel: 069 618 633. Good value local favourite on the old town square, near the clock tower, reasonably priced and always packed. Grilled meat and fish, soups, *japraci* and stuffed peppers, salads and other dishes. **€**

**Stara Kuća** *Iva Andrića 5;* www.starakuca.me. North of the city centre near the Hotel Piramida, with – as the name suggests – a rustic stone and wood interior (Stara Kuća means 'the old house'). Grilled meat and fish, veal and lamb cooked *ispod sač*, plus pasta dishes and risotto. **€€**

# KOTOR

**BBQ Tanjga** Šuranj bb; tel: 069 863 836. Between the bus station and the old town, this unassuming little place serves up very good grilled meat (steak, *ćevapčići*, *ražnjići*), served with roast potatoes or chips, *ajvar*, delicious roasted or grilled vegetables and simple, fresh salads. Very much a local place, good value, friendly and unpretentious. **€**

**Galion** Šuranj bb; www.galion.me. Upmarket restaurant outside the old city walls, which usually tops the list for fine dining in Kotor, and with prices considerably higher than most other places. Tables are right on the waterfront, in a modern, glass-enclosed terrace overlooking the superyachts moored on the Bay of Kotor. Reservations recommended. **€€€**

**Giardino** Stari Grad 350, Kotor old town; tel: 069 618 132. Restaurant/pizzeria in the old town, on the corner of Trg Bokeljske Mornarice opposite the Maritime Museum. Seafood, grills and pizzas with friendly service at reasonable prices. **€€**

**Konoba Bonaca** Dobrota 170; www.facebook.com/konobabonacakotor. Don't let the stupendous bay views distract you from the great food at this waterfront tavern. Known for its seafood and knowledgeable service. **€€**

**Konoba Cesarica** Stari Grad 375, Kotor old town; tel: 069 049 733. Just off St Luke's Square, this spot has an attractive interior with heavy bench-style wooden tables under a vaulted brick ceiling. Good seafood including grilled sea bass, grilled squid, octopus salad, mussels and fried whitebait. Friendly service. **€€**

**Konoba Galerija** Šuranj bb; tel: 069 811 801. Outside the city walls, near Galion but more relaxed and with fewer pretentions and much lower prices. Nice terrace. Seafood and grills. **€€**

**Konoba Roma** Pijaca od salate; tel: 067 504 064. Next to the better-known Konoba Scala Santa, but more low key and with lower prices. The usual Montenegrin fare – seafood, grills, risotto – in a lovely location, with friendly service. **€€**

**Pizzeria Pronto** Kotor old town; tel: 067 991 666. Tiny pizzeria on a narrow street near Hotel Vardar, with just half a dozen tables under a vaulted ceiling. Good value, and popular – but if you can't get a table, they naturally also do take-away. Hands down the best pizza in town. **€**

# AROUND THE BAY OF KOTOR

**Bocalibre €** Perast seafront; tel: 068 825 445. Multitasking seafront Italian café-restaurant that's as good for a pastry and espresso breakfast as it is for an evening pizza blow-out. The latter comes in for much praise. **€**

**Konoba Čatovića Mlini €€€** Morinj; www.catovica-mlini.com. An old stone mill (*mlin* in Montenegrin), which has been in the current owner's family for some 200 years, converted into a *konoba*. Enjoy seafood, traditional local dishes and homemade wine in a beautiful stone interior with wooden beams, or out on a large terrace. Dishes include fish baked in salt, octopus fried in polenta and wild asparagus salad. Lovely riverside setting. Credit cards accepted. Reservations recommended. **€€€**

**Konoba Feral €€** Šetalište 5 Danica 47, Herceg Novi; www.konobaferal.com. For a traditional and unpretentious *konoba* renowned for its exceptionally good, fresh seafood, the Montenegrin coast doesn't get much better than this. Also serves pasta, risottos and other dishes. On the waterfront below the old town. Very popular. **€€**

**Pod Lozom €** Trg N Djurkovića bb, Herceg Novi; tel: 031 322 800. Great little local favourite on the north side of the main square in Herceg Novi, with tables outside on the square in a covered area. Grills, seafood, *japra-*

*ci*, stuffed peppers and other vegetarian dishes. Friendly service and good value. **€**

## TIVAT

**Bokka** Villa Teuta Porto Montenegro, www.instagram.com/bokka_modern. The upmarket dining experience is second to none in this area of Montenegro. Gourmet dishes are paired with local wines. Reservations essential. **€€**

**One** Porto Montenegro; www.facebook.com/jettyone. Upmarket brasserie located by Porto Montenegro's Jetty #1, a light and airy space with a nice terrace. **€€€**

## SOUTH COAST

**Jadran kod Krsta** Obala bb, Budva; www.restaurantjadran.me. Long-established (it was opened in the 1970s), popular seafood restaurant with a lovely vine-covered terrace and tables right on the waterfront, near the marina. Also serves steaks and other grills. **€€€**

**Konoba Bocun** Ulica Mimoza 177, Budva; www.konobabocun.com. This well-kept, family-run tavern does everything from a simple omelette to a fish and seafood platter for two. Lots of fresh salads, grilled meats and hearty soups. **€-€€**

**Parma** Mainski put 70, Budva; tel: 067 573 733. Away from the tourist hotspots of the old town and the beach, just north of Obilaznica žrtava fašizma, this unpretentious local favourite serves very good value grilled meat (*ćevapčići*, *ražnjići*, *pljeskavica* and so on) in a low-key, tavern-like setting. **€**

**Restoran Lim** Slovenska plaža, Budva; tel: 067 371 911. Popular seafood restaurant on the waterfront, with a nice terrace surrounded by trees and shrubs. Fish, shellfish, steaks and salads. **€€**

**Royal Garden Juice Bar** Vranjak 13, Budva old town; tel: 067 344 555. Freshly-squeezed juices, sandwiches, salads, soups and other light bites, as well as cakes and breakfasts. A good choice for vegetarians. **€**

## SVETI STEFAN

**Drago** Slobode 32; http://restaurantdrago.com. Under the apartments of the same name, this long-established restaurant serves grilled and roast meat, seafood, stews, pizza and salads. Lovely leafy terrace, beautifully presented food, friendly staff and reasonable prices. **€€**

## BAR AND ULCINJ

**Kaldrma** Ulica 9. Januar, Stari Bar; tel: 067 988 903. Lovely little restaurant/café on the steep cobbled street leading up beside the old town, with outdoor seating and a nice light-flooded room on the first floor. Local cheese and olives, veal with aubergine. Good vegetarian options such as roasted aubergine with cheese, stuffed vine leaves, tasty salads. Some mouthwatering deserts and rich, dark Turkish coffee. Relaxed, friendly service and good value.

**La Tavola** Ulica Hafiz Ali Ulqinaku (this street is also known as 26 Novembar), Ulcinj; tel: 069 102 010. This smart, glass-fronted restaurant with bright interior and tables out on the street is both popular and good value. Serves grills, seafood, pasta and pizza. **€€**

**Miško** Ada Bojana, Ulcinj; tel: 069 022 868. Long-established seafood restaurant, very highly regarded. Nice wood-ceilinged terrace right beside the River Bojana. **€€€**

**Restoran Knjaževa Bašta** Dvorac Kralja Nikole, Bar; www.knjazevabasta.com. Steaks, grilled fish, stuffed veal fillets, mussels *na buzari* and other dishes in a particularly elegant setting – a 19th century glass conservatory, part of a complex built at the order of King Nikola and originally surrounded by lush tropical gardens. Good service and reasonable prices. **€€**

**Taphana** Ulcinj, old town; www.facebook.com/RestaurantTaphana. Nice setting with terrace on the edge of the old town, with good sunset views. Seafood and grills at reasonable prices, and pleasant service. **€€**

## CETINJE

**Restoran Kole** Crnogorskih Junaka 12; http://restaurantkole.me. Central, upmarket restaurant, with a somewhat gaudy interior (think purple chairs, yellow walls) but good food and service. Dishes include grilled or boiled meat, beef goulash, veal *paprikaš*, carp, trout, *kastradina* and *kačamak*. Popular with wedding receptions. **€€**

**Restoran Konak** Zabrdje bb; www.konak.me. Four kilometres (2.5 miles) south of Cetinje on the main road to Budva, this restaurant serves excellent traditional Montenegrin dishes, including lamb cooked *ispod sač*, grilled meat, freshwater fish (carp, trout) and seafood, as well as vegetarian dishes and homemade bread. There is a rustic interior and a big terrace. There are plans to open a botanical garden next to the restaurant, with alpine plants from Lovćen, Orjen and other mountains along the coast. Credit cards accepted. Coach tours sometimes stop here so it's worth reserving a table. **€€**

**Restoran TavèRna** Cetinje; tel: 069 502 503. Good value pizzas and grills, as well as traditional dishes such as *kačamak*, marinated carp salad, beef goulash and some pasta dishes. Stone interior with polished wooden floors and tables on the street outside. Credit cards accepted. **€€**

## LAKE SKADAR

**Godinje Tavern** Godinje; tel: 067 308 664. In the tiny, mostly abandoned village of Godinje on the hillside above Lake Skadar, this tavern offers traditional local dishes and award-winning homemade wine. **€**

**Konoba Mostina** Rijeka Crnojevića; tel: 069 843 317; www.mostina.me. Located right by the iconic 19th century triple-arched stone bridge which spans the River Crnojevića just before it broadens and flows into Lake Skadar, in a restored stone house built at the same time as the bridge. Dishes include marinated smoked carp, eel risotto, duck risotto, grilled trout and wild boar goulash. Riverside terrace. Good, friendly service and reasonable prices make this the best place to eat at Rijeka Crnojevića. **€€**

**Stari Most** Rijeka Crnojevića; tel: 067 339 429. Upscale restaurant serving traditional Montenegrin dishes, near the old bridge, though some reviews suggest it may be resting on its laurels somewhat. Typical dishes include marinated smoked carp and eel in rice with dried plums. Reservations recommended. **€€€**

## DURMITOR AND THE NORTHWEST

**Dvorište** Jakova Ostoji a, Žabljak; tel: 068 497 173. Cosy spot in an old stone house in Žabljak where you can enjoy traditional local cuisine and beer after a day on the trails. **€€**

**Restoran Durmitor** Ulica Božidara Žugića bb, Žabljak; tel: 069 637 316. In the centre of town, try this spot for Durmitor steak, *ćevapčići* and other grilled dishes at reasonable prices, in a simple, partly wood-panelled interior. **€**

**Restaurant Or'O** Njegoševa, Žabljak; tel +069 406 210. A cosy spot clad-ded in wood throughout. There's also a lovely terrace for early evening drinks. Great local produce and traditional dishes, and a fantastic wine list to boot. **€€**

**Restoran Vodenica** Kolašin; tel: 069 241 507. Grilled meat and freshwater fish, and traditional dishes such as *kačamak* and *cicvara* served in a cosy, wood-panelled interior, within an old water mill. On the north side of town beside the river. **€€**

**Zlatni bor** Tmajevci bb, Žabljak; www.hotelzlatnibor.com. The interior has a wood-panelled ceiling, while the walls are decorated with old farming implements and shepherd's shears, and there's a nice covered terrace. Typical Montenegrin fare at reasonable prices, 1km (0.6 mile) northeast of the town centre, part of the hotel of the same name. **€€**

## PROKLETIJE AND THE NORTHEAST

**Kula Damjanova** Vojno Selo, Plav; www.kuladamjanova.com. Venture 1.5km (1 mile) south of the town centre to the stone-built hotel of the same name. Rustic, tavern-like setting with a roaring hearth in winter and hearty mountain dishes including game, as well as grilled meat and fish. **€**

# Travel essentials

## PRACTICAL INFORMATION


Accessible travel 126
Accommodation 126
Airports 127
Apps 128
Bicycle hire 128
Budgeting for your trip 128
Camping 128
Car rental 128
Climate 129
Crime and safety 129
Driving 130
Electricity 130
Embassies 130
Emergencies 131
Getting there 131
Guides and tours 131
Health and medical care 132
Language 132
LGBTQI+ Travel 135
Money 135
Opening times 136
Public holidays 136
Religion 137
Telephones 137
Time zones 137
Tipping 137
Toilets 138
Tourist information 138
Transport 138
Visas and entry requirements 139

# ACCESSIBLE TRAVEL

Montenegro is not the most disability-friendly country in Europe and those with mobility problems should check ahead whether they are likely to encounter problems with stairs etc. Some hotels on the coast may now have a few rooms with disabled facilities. Globtour Montenegro (www.globtour-montenegro.com) offer tours designed specifically for those with disabilities.

# ACCOMMODATION

**Hotels.** Hotels are classified by stars (five stars down to zero), but the fact that one hotel has more stars than another is not always a reliable indication of whether it's a nicer place to stay. Stars are awarded primarily in accordance with facilities, such as a restaurant, conference hall or swimming pool, rather than room quality or taste, or for that matter, service – all of which may well be better at a particular three-star hotel than at a nearby hotel with four or five stars.

Some hotels and other accommodation providers close for the winter between November and March, while in July and August, accommodation in popular spots on the coast can get heavily booked, so it's worth reserving in advance. In the summer, there may be a surcharge for stays of fewer than three nights.

**Rooms *(sobe)* and apartments.** These are offered widely in Montenegro, particularly on the coast, and are in general cheaper and better value than hotels. A *soba* is a guestroom in someone's house – something like a bed and breakfast, without the breakfast – while an apartment (*apartman*) will have a kitchen, and generally costs a little more than a *soba* (but may sleep more people). In peak season, apartments in particular may only be offered on a seven night basis. People offering rooms or apartments may still wait at bus and train stations, sometimes with photos to show of the accommodation on offer. If you find a place you're interested in, make sure you understand the price (including whether there's a surcharge if you're just staying for one or two nights) and how far it is from the town centre, before accepting. However, these days most people book through popular short-term rentals sites such as Airbnb and Booking.com.

**Agrotourism and eco-resorts.** These are increasingly offered in rural areas and can provide a more authentic experience than a large resort-style hotel. They are particularly good along the Peaks of the Balkans Trail.

## AIRPORTS

Montenegro has two international airports, Podgorica near the capital and Tivat on the coast.

**Podgorica Airport** (IATA Code TGR; www.montenegroairports.com - also known as **Golubovci Airport**) lies some 11km (7 miles) south of Podgorica near the suburb of Golubovci, on the road to Virpazar and Petrovac na Moru.

The easiest way to get to Podgorica from the airport is by taxi – licensed taxis wait outside the arrivals hall, with a journey into the centre of Podgorica costing from €15 (but if you book a taxi in advance, it will cost less, usually no more than €10 for up to four passengers – there are plenty of taxi companies to choose from, with TaxiTravel being one of the cheapest: tel: +382 (0)69 949 197, www.taxi-travel.me).

There's also a bus into the centre of Podgorica, line L20, which departs from opposite arrivals seven times daily between and stops at the bus station, at Most Braće Zlatičanin and Bul Stanka Dragojevića (for Trg Republika) before continuing to Hram. A ticket costs €2 and can be bought from the driver.

**Tivat Airport** (IATA Code TIV; www.montenegroairports.com) is located around 3km (1.8 miles) south of Tivat, between the Bay of Kotor and the Luštica peninsula. Tivat Airport receives the bulk of high season and charter flights to Montenegro, however there is no bus service, so you'll need to get a taxi (from €15).

For many years the most convenient and popular way to get to Montenegro was to fly to **Dubrovnik Airport** (IATA Code DBV; www.airport-dubrovnik.hr) just 29km (18 miles) from Herceg Novi over the border at Čilipi in Croatia, with Dubrovnik itself lying a further 20km (12.4 miles) along the coast. If you take a taxi from the airport to Herceg Novi *don't* get a taxi only to the border, as there's no public transport from there and – particularly if travelling towards Čilipi – you'll be charged a premium rate for a taxi from there. There's a regular bus from the airport into Dubrovnik, and a regular bus from Dubrovnik to Montenegro, via Herceg Novi and Kotor and then going to either Podgorica or Ulcinj (5 services daily in each direction, for timetables and tickets see flixbus.com).

## APPS

International taxi apps such as Uber and Bolt aren't available in Montenegro. However, the TeslaGoApp (https://teslaclub.me/en) has a fleet of electric vehicles you can book. Other useful apps include Moovit (https://moovitapp.com), which helps you plan journeys on the local public transport system.

## BICYCLE HIRE

There are plenty of places on the Montenegrin coast as well as inland offering bicycle hire, and a good network of mountain bike trails has been developed, many of them marked with yellow signs.

Main roads are less suitable for cycling, the main coastal highway in particular which sees an enormous volume of traffic in the summer, and which tends to drive alarmingly fast.

## BUDGETING FOR YOUR TRIP

Montenegro is relatively cheap to travel in compared to Western Europe, though price hikes and inflation have increased the cost of holidaying here immensely. In general, prices are higher on the coast, and (with the exception of the capital Podgorica which caters more to business than budget travellers), lower inland.

## CAMPING

Wild camping, including in national parks and nature reserves, as well as on the coast, is illegal in Montenegro. There are large campsites catering to campervans as well as tents along the coast, and a few designated camping areas for hikers carrying tents in the mountains, including Durmitor and other national parks. Anyone camping at the latter should be aware of the extreme risk posed by wildfires, and exercise caution use camping stoves. Never light an open fire in the wild.

## CAR RENTAL (see also Driving)

There are car hire offices in Podgorica as well as the main towns along the coast, and desks at both Podgorica and Tivat airports. It's always more reliable (and cheaper) to book in advance, and this becomes more or less essential in the summer. The airport desks may only be open for pre-booked cars.

Reputable local agencies include Meridian (www.meridian-rentacar.com) which has offices at Podgorica Airport, Tivat Airport, as well as in Podgorica, Budva and Bar; and Delta (www.rentacar-delta.com) which has offices in Podgorica as well as at Podgorica Airport and Tivat Airport .

Expect to pay around €50 per day for a small car in peak season. There are also larger international companies, the prices of which tend to be higher or lower depending how and when you book.

## CLIMATE

Montenegro's climate is Mediterranean along the coast, Continental inland. On the coast, you can expect an average summer maximum of 31°C (89°F), dropping to an average summer minimum of 18°C (64°F). Summer humidity can reach uncomfortable levels. Rain on the coast falls mainly in the winter (November generally sees the highest rainfall). Inland in the north of the country, summer maximum and minimum figures tend to be around 5 degrees less than those given above, and in winter don't get much above freezing – and once you get into the mountains themselves, they will be considerably lower, with heavy snowfall in winter.

Podgorica had the distinction of registering the highest summer temperatures of anywhere in the former Yugoslavia, while Orjen, a mountain near the coast near the border with Croatia, has some of the highest recorded rainfall of anywhere in Europe.

## CRIME AND SAFETY

Montenegro is a relatively safe country to travel in, and the crime rate including theft is quite low. This should not however preclude the usual precautions, such as not leaving your belongings unattended (in particular, don't leave valuables unattended on the beach), or waving large wads of cash around. Watch out for scams and tricksters, especially where Serbs and Russians holiday (such as Herceg Novi).

## DRIVING

**Road conditions.** Roads in Montenegro are a mixed bag and can be rough and steep away from the main routes (which are now pretty well-maintained). As well as uneven changes in surface, roads are often narrow and winding; expect a few rocks and potholes if you head off on back-country roads. Locals tend to drive fast, and caution is advised when driving in Montenegro. Road signs are in the Latin alphabet.

**Rules and regulations.** In Montenegro you drive on the right. Drivers must be over 18 and in possession of a valid driving licence (UK citizens should check what licence they currently need – EU driving licences are fine). Speed limits are 80km/h on motorways, 50km/h in towns or built up areas, seat belts must be worn, and headlights must be switched on (dipped) at all times. The maximum blood alcohol limit is 0.02. Having a reflective jacket in the car, and putting it on if you get out of the car in the advent of a breakdown or emergency, is mandatory.

**Breakdowns and emergencies.** In the advent of a breakdown or emergency, you are required to use a warning triangle and wear a reflective jacket when out of the car. Don't leave the scene of the accident until the police have arrived. The Automobile Association of Montenegro (AMSCG, www.amscg.org) provides emergency roadside assistance.

## ELECTRICITY

220V/50Hz. Sockets are European standard round two-pin.

## EMBASSIES

The UK and US as well as many European countries have embassies in Podgorica:

**UK:** British Embassy, Ulcinjska 8, Gorica C, 81000 Podgorica; tel: 020 618 010; www.gov.uk/government/world/organisations/british-embassy-podgorica.

**US:** US Embassy, Dzona Dzeksona 2, 81000 Podgorica; tel: 020 410 500; http://podgorica.usembassy.gov.

## EMERGENCIES

The following emergency telephone numbers are valid in Montenegro:

**Emergency** (through which calls will be routed to the appropriate fire, police or ambulance services by an operator) 112

**Police** 122

**Fire** 123

**Ambulance** 124

## GETTING THERE

**By air.** Most 'budget' airlines have year-round flights to Podgorica and perhaps seasonal services to Tivat. Flying to Dubrovnik provides you with vastly more options. Using Belgrade as an access point is not advised. When searching for flights online, always check the 'flag carriers' as these can now be cheaper than so-called 'budget' operators, especially if you have luggage.

**By rail.** The port of Bar on the Montenegrin coast lies at the end of the spectacular Belgrade–Bar railway line, on which there's one daily service plus one night train in each direction. Note that there is no railway line along the coast. Both Serbia and Montenegro are included in the Interrail network.

**By sea.** There are ferry routes from Bar to Bari with Montenegro Lines (www.montenegrolines.com); however, there are numerous reports of unclean beds and toilets, and bookings for cabins not honoured.

## GUIDES AND TOURS

British couple Ben and Emma Heywood of **Undiscovered Montenegro** (tel: +44 (0)20 3287 0015; www.undiscoveredmontenegro.com) offer their guests an outstanding choice of excursions and activities on and around Lake Skadar, from their beautifully renovated stone guesthouse Villa Miela near Virpazar, which they have made their home since 2008. They can organise activities from kayaking on Lake Skadar to hiking in the local mountains, plus wine tours, foodie extravaganzas and yoga retreats.

**Montenegro Holiday** (email: info@montenegroholiday.com; www.montenegroholiday.com) is an online-based company run by British couple Hayley and Jack Wright, who have lived in Herceg Novi for 10 years and were the first UK outfit to begin specialising in active/outdoor trips in Montenegro. Hiking, mountaineering, mountain biking and rafting trips all over the country are on offer, as well as cultural tours and scuba diving.

## HEALTH AND MEDICAL CARE

Montenegro has a reciprocal agreement entitling citizens of the UK and some other nations to free emergency healthcare treatment. You will need to show your passport to obtain this service. Otherwise, there is a network of private clinics, including:

CODRA: Ulica Radosava Burića Pod Lipović, 81000 Podgorica; tel: +382 (0)20 648 334; www.codrahospital.me

Bolnica Meljine: Braće Grakalića 94-100, 85340 Herceg Novi; tel: +382 (0)31 640 988; www.bolnica-meljine.me

There are pharmacies in most towns of any size (look for a sign saying *apoteka*). There's a useful list of Montefarm-owned pharmacies across the country, with contact details, on the company website (www.montefarm.co.me and click on Apoteke).

Make sure you carry sunscreen and a sunhat in Montenegro, as well as some form of insect repellent as mosquitoes are widespread (and voracious). If you're hiking, it's worth knowing that ticks are also present in Montenegro (as they are in much of Europe), and in some cases may carry a risk of Lyme disease and European tick-borne encephalitis. It is therefore wise to carry a small tick removing tool such as the O'Tom Tick Twister (www.ticktwister.co.uk) – if you find a tick on you, slip the head of the tool under the tick's body, as close to your skin as possible, and twist gently (do *not* pull, squeeze or crush the tick's abdomen, or try to dislodge it with irritants, as this will cause it to regurgitate and therefore increase the risk of infection).

# LANGUAGE

The language spoken in Montenegro is Serbian *(srpski)*, but since independence from Serbia in 2006 has been called Montenegrin *(crnogorski)* in Montenegro. Montenegrin is written in both the Latin and Cyrillic alphabets, with menus and many other things you might find yourself needing to read usually written in the former. Serbian is a South Slavonic language, very similar though not quite the same as Croatian and Bosnian, and along with Croatian formed the base of the amalgamated, or 'standardised' language spoken in the former Yugoslavia, called Serbo-Croat.

English is spoken widely in places generally visited by tourists (French, German and Italian are also widely spoken), especially along the coast, although this is usually not the case in small villages far off the established tourist trail.

Several letters in the Montenegrin alphabet are pronounced differently to how they would be pronounced in English – particular ones to look out for are c (pronounced ts) and j (pronounced y).

The following table lists all 30 letters of the Montenegrin alphabet in both Latin and Cyrillic form, along with the closest pronunciation to which they correspond in English. There is no q, w, x or y in the Montenegrin alphabet (except in foreign words and names).

| Latin | **Cyrillic** | Equivalent sound in English |
|---|---|---|
| A a | **А а** | as the 'a' in father |
| B b | **Б б** | same as in English |
| C c | **Ц ц** | as the 'ts' in cats |
| Č č | **Ч ч** | as the 'ch' in church |
| Ć ć | **Ћ ћ** | as the 'tch' in picture |
| D d | **Д д** | same as in English |
| Đ đ | **Ђ ђ** | as the 'dj' in duke |
| Dž dž | **Џ џ** | as the 'j' in jam |
| E e | **Е е** | as the 'e' in egg |
| F f | **Ф ф** | same as in English |
| G g | **Г г** | as the 'g' in give |

| | | |
|---|---|---|
| H h | **Х х** | same as in English |
| I i | **И и** | as the 'i' in ill |
| J j | **J j** | as the 'y' in yes |
| K k | **К k** | same as in English |
| L l | **Л л** | same as in English |
| Lj lj | **Љ љ** | as the 'lli' in million |
| M m | **М m** | same as in English |
| N n | **Н н** | same as in English |
| Nj nj | **Њ њ** | as the 'ni' in onion |
| O o | **О о** | as the 'o' in hot |
| P p | **П п** | same as in English |
| R r | **Р р** | same as in English, but rolled slightly |
| S s | **С с** | same as in English |
| Š š | **Ш ш** | as the 'sh' in shake |
| T t | **Т т** | same as in English |
| U u | **У у** | as the 'oo' in pool |
| V v | **В в** | same as in English |
| Z z | **З з** | same as in English |
| Ž ž | **Ж ж** | as the 's' in measure |

**Greetings and basic phrases**

Hello/Good day **Dobar dan**

Good morning **Dobro jutro**

Good evening **Dobro veče**

Hi! **Ćao!**

Goodbye **Do viđenja**

Yes **Da**

No **Ne**

Please **Molim**

Thank you **Hvala**

You're welcome **Molim**

Sorry! **Izvinite!**

Excuse me… (when about to request something) **Oprostite…**
Where is…? **Gdje je…?**
Do you speak English? **Da li govorite engleski?**
I don't understand. **Ne razumijem.**
I don't know Cyrillic. **Ja ne znam ćirilicu.**
Please could I have… **Molim vas…**
How much does it cost? **Koliko košta?**
Do you have a single/double room? **Da li imate jednokrevetnu/dvokrevetnu sobu?**
One ticket/Two tickets to… please. **Jednu kartu/Dvije karte do… molim.**

## LGBTQI+ TRAVEL

Montenegro remains a conservative society, and is not particularly tolerant towards homosexuality. Locals who are gay live in a culture of concealment and keep their sexuality well hidden. There are no openly (or even covertly) gay or lesbian bars or clubs in Montenegro. The premises of LGBTQI+ organisations in Podgorica have been attacked on several occasions. Exercise caution – avoid overt displays of same-sex affection. Booking rooms for same sex couples is not, however, usually a problem.

## MONEY

**Currency.** Montenegro adopted the euro in 2002. Notes come in denominations of 5, 10, 20, 50, 100 and (rare)200 euros; coins have denominations of 1, 2, 5, 10, 20 and 50 cents, and there are also 1 and 2 euro coins.

**Currency exchange.** The best place to exchange foreign currency is at exchange offices (*mjenjačnica*). You can also exchange foreign currency at some bank branches (*banka*), but the queues will be longer and you won't get a better rate than at an exchange office, and the range of currencies accepted is likely to be smaller.

**ATMs.** ATMs (*bankomat*) are widespread in major towns and cities, where most bank branches will have one. This remains the most convenient way to carry cash in Montenegro, taking out enough for a few days at a time. Small villages generally won't have an ATM, so if travelling in rural areas, make sure you have enough cash with you to cover this part of your trip.

**Credit cards.** Credit and debit cards are accepted widely at larger hotels, supermarkets and elsewhere, though for private rooms you'll generally need to pay in cash. Visa and MasterCard are the most commonly accepted; Amex and Diners less so.

## OPENING TIMES

Banking hours vary from place to place in Montenegro, but in general banks are open Monday to Friday 8am–8pm, Saturday 8am–1pm. Shops are usually open Monday to Saturday 9am–8pm, sometimes from a couple of hours earlier. Larger supermarkets are likely to be open on Sunday, smaller shops will probably be closed. Museum hours vary (and lack of funding may mean you find them closed), but are generally open Tuesday to Sunday.

## PUBLIC HOLIDAYS

Official public holidays in Montenegro, where everything will be shut and a reduced (Sunday) timetable will be in place for buses etc, are:

**1–2 January** New Year

**7 January** Orthodox Christmas Day

**March/April/May** Orthodox Easter

**1–2 May** Labour Day

**9 May** Victory in Europe Day

**21–2 May** Independence Day (commemorating Montenegro's referendum for independence in 2006)

**13–14 July** Statehood Day (commemorating the recognition of Montenegro as an independent state at the Congress of Berlin in 1878)

**29–30 November** Republic Day

**25 December** Christmas Day

Movable official holidays include Good Friday and Easter Monday, and other major religious holidays such as Whit Monday (Pentecost, 50 days after Easter Sunday) and All Saints (1 November) may also be observed.

Holidays are celebrated over two days, and moved to the following Monday and Tuesday if they fall at weekends.

## RELIGION

The population of Montenegro belong primarily to the Orthodox Church (around 72 percent), with a sizeable Muslim minority (around 19 percent) concentrated mainly in the southeast of the country, near the border with Albania, and Roman Catholics making up a little over 3 percent of the population.

## TELEPHONES

The international code for Montenegro is +382.

Local area codes are three digits, including an initial zero which is omitted if calling from abroad or from an overseas mobile. Some of the main area codes are:

Podgorica: 020
Bar, Ulcinj: 030
Herceg Novi: 031
Kotor, Tivat: 032
Budva: 033
Cetinje: 041
Plav: 051
Žabljak: 052

As Montenegro is not a member of the EU, roaming charges may still apply. Check with your operator whether you will be charged for using your phone in Montenegro.

## TIME ZONES

Montenegro lies within the Central European Time Zone (CET) – that is, one hour ahead of Greenwich Mean Time – and observes Daylight Saving.

| New York | London | **Montenegro** | Jo'burg | Sydney | Auckland |
|---|---|---|---|---|---|
| 6am | 11am | **noon** | 1pm | 8pm | 10pm |

## TIPPING

Tipping is not compulsory, but if you feel the service in a restaurant deserves it, leaving a small amount – 5 percent of the bill, or one or two euro coins – will be appreciated. Many now simply round up the bill to the nearest five or ten euros. Taxi drivers are not usually tipped, nor hotel staff, with the possible exception of at more upmarket or exclusive resorts.

## TOILETS

Public toilets do exist in major tourist centres but are relatively scarce, with the exception of bus and train stations (where entering the toilets usually costs around 50 cents). The standard of public toilets may not be great either. Restaurants, larger cafés and museums have toilets. Waste pipes are usually narrow and are easily clogged, so where indicated put toilet paper in the waste bin provided rather than down the toilet.

## TOURIST INFORMATION

Montenegro National Tourist Office:
Ulica Slobode 2, 81000 Podgorica; tel: +382 (0)77 100 001; www.montenegro.travel
Contact details for some of the main local tourist offices are:
Budva Tourist Office: Mediteranska 8/6, 85310 Budva; tel: +382 (0)33 402 814; www.budva.travel
Kotor Tourist Office: Stari grad 315, 85330 Kotor; tel: +382 (0)32 325 947 or +382 (0)32 325 950; www.tokotor.me
Podgorica Tourist Office: Ulica Slobode 47, 81000 Podgorica; tel: +382 (0)20 667 535; www.podgorica.travel

## TRANSPORT

**Bus.** Travelling by bus is the most common means of public transport in Montenegro, both between different parts of the country and within larger urban areas such as Podgorica. Services vary in frequency from every hour or so between towns along the coast and between Podgorica and the coast, to just four or five services a day between Podgorica and towns further inland such as Plav.

Bus services are operated by several private companies. For schedules and tickets try (www.busticket4.me).

**Train.** Until recently, the only passenger rail route in Montenegro was the line running from Bar on the coast to Belgrade in Serbia, via the following towns in Montenegro: Virpazar, Podgorica, Mojkovac and Bijelo Polje. There are two departures each day in either direction between Bar and Bijeljo Polje (continuing to Belgrade) plus another between Podgorica and Bijelo Polje, and another seven between Bar and Podgorica. Journey times are around 1 hour between Podgorica and Bar and 2 hours 30 mins between Podgorica and Bijelo Polje. The line between Podgorica and Nikšić opened to passenger trains a few years ago and there are now about 10 services a day in either direction, with a journey time of around 80 mins.

Trains are operated by Montenegrin Railways (Željeznički prevoz Crne Gore, www.zcg-prevoz.me), which has a website in English.

**Taxi.** Taxis in Montenegro (both within and between towns) are relatively cheap, though most towns are small enough to negotiate on foot. Fares within towns should be metered; longer journeys such as from the airport or to another city tend to be for a set price which should be agreed in advance (many companies have prices listed on their website).

## VISAS AND ENTRY REQUIREMENTS

British and other EU citizens, as well as citizens of the US, Canada, Australia and New Zealand, do not need a visa to enter Montenegro as a tourist, and can stay for up to 90 days. Other nationals, including citizens of South Africa, are required to obtain a visa before travelling to Montenegro. There is a list of visa requirements for individual countries on the website of the Ministry of Foreign Affairs and European Integration: www.gov.me/en/diplomatic-missions/embassies-and-consulates-of-montenegro.

All foreigners entering Montenegro are required to register with the police within 24 hours, but providing you are staying at a hotel, room or apartment or other licensed accommodation, your host will do that automatically when they take your passport details.

# Index


## A
Ada Bojana 67
Alan Ford 36

## B
Bar 64
Bay of Kotor 43
Biogradska Gora National Park 86
Bjelasica 87
Budva 59
- beaches 62
- Church of St John 61
- Church of St Mary in Punta 61
- Church of the Holy Trinity 61
- Citadel 61
- City Museum 61
- City of Theatre Festival 61
- Modern Gallery 61
- old town 60

## C
Cetinje 68
- Art Museum 70
- Church of the Birth of Our Lady 70
- Ethnographic Museum 71
- King Nikola's Museum 71
- Lapidarium 71
- Monastery 69
- National Museum of Montenegro 70
- Njegoš Museum at Biljarda 71
- Orlov Krš 72

## D
Dioclea 37
Dobrota 47
Durmitor National Park 82

## F
Fašinada 47

## G
Grbaja Valley 91
Gusinje 90

## H
Herceg Novi 39
- Church of St Jerome 41
- Church of the Archangel Michael 40
- Citadela 42
- Clock Tower 40
- Forte Mare 41
- Kanli Kula 39
- Savina Monastery 42
- Španjola 40
- Trg Nikole Đurkovića 40

Hridsko jezero 89

## I
Ivanova korita 74

## K
Kamenari 44
Kolašin 87
Kosmač 62
Kotor 48
- Bishopric 56
- Cathedral of St Tryphon 52
- Chapel of Our Lady of Health 50
- Clock Tower 52
- Drago Palace 55
- Duke's Palace 52
- Karampana Fountain 56
- Maritime Museum 55
- market 56
- Pima Palace 55
- St Clare's Church 54
- St John's Fort 50
- St Luke's Church 54
- St Mary's Church 54
- St Michael's Church 54
- Trg od Oružja 51

## L
Lake Piva 81
Lake Skadar 75
Lipci 44
Lovćen 72
- national park 74
- Njegoš Mausoleum 73

Luštica Peninsula 58

## M
Mamula 59
Medun 37
Miljanov, Marko 38
Mojkovac 86
Monastery of St George 46
Morača Monastery 87

**N**

Njeguši 74

**O**

Orjen 43
Ostrog Monastery 81
Ottoman fort 78
Our Lady of the Rocks 46

**P**

Peaks of the Balkans Trail 91
Perast 45
- Church of St Nicholas 45
- Town Museum 46

Petrovac na Moru 63
Plav 88
Plužine 81
Podgorica 34
- City Museum 36
- Clock Tower 37
- Gallery of Modern Art 36
- Gorica 35, 37
- Millenium Bridge 35
- Natural History Museum 36
- old stone bridge 37
- Orthodox Cathedral of the Resurrection of Christ and the Church of the Holy Savior 36
- Petrović Palace 36
- Roman Catholic Church of the Sacred Heart of Jesus 36
- Skender Čaušin Mosque 37
- St George's Church 36
- Trg Republika 37

Prčanj 48
Prčanj Church of the Birth of Our Lady 48
Prokletije National Park 90

**R**

Raška Style 86
Rijeka Crnojevića 79
Risan 44
River Bojana 67
Rumija 79

**S**

Šćepan Polje 81
Solila 58
Stari Bar 65
St Nikola Island 62
Sv Stefan 62

**T**

Tara Bridge 85
Tara Canyon 83
Tivat 57
- Buća Palace 57
- City Park 57
- Donja Lastva 58
- Gornja Lastva 58
- Porto Montenegro 57

**U**

Ulcinj 65
- Church-Mosque 65
- Museum of Ulcinj 66
- Namazgjahu Mosque 66
- old town 65
- Orthodox Cathedral of St Nicholas 66
- Pasha Mosque 66

Ulcinj Salina 67

**V**

Velika plaža 66
Verige 44
Via Dinarica 91
Virpazar 77
Visitorsko jezero 90

**Z**

Žabljak 83

# BENEFITS OF PLANNING AND BOOKING AT ROUGHGUIDES.COM/TRIPS

### PLAN YOUR ADVENTURE WITH LOCAL EXPERTS

Rough Guides' English-speaking local experts are hand-picked, based on their experience in the travel industry and their impeccable standards of customer service.

### SAVE TIME AND GET ACCESS TO LOCAL KNOWLEDGE

When a local expert plans your trip, you save time and money when you book, even during high season. You won't be charged for using a credit card either.

### MAKE TRAVEL A BREEZE: BOOK WITH PEACE OF MIND

Enjoy stress-free travel when you use Rough Guides' secure online booking platform. All bookings come with a money-back guarantee.

## WHAT DO OTHER TRAVELLERS THINK ABOUT ROUGH GUIDES TRIPS?

This Spain tour company did a fantastic job to make our dream trip perfect. We gave them our travel budget, told them where we would like to go, and they did all of the planning. Our drivers and tour guides were always on time and very knowledgable. The hotel accommodations were better than we would have found on our own. Only one time did we end up in a location that we had not intended to be in. We called the 24 hour phone number, and they immediately fixed the situation.

**Don A, USA**

## PLAN AND BOOK YOUR TRIP AT ROUGHGUIDES.COM/TRIPS

# THE **MINI** ROUGH GUIDE TO **MONTENEGRO**

**First edition 2025**

**Editor:** Beth Williams
**Author:** Marc di Duca
**Picture Editor:** Piotr Kala
**Picture Manager:** Tom Smyth
**Cartography Update:** Katie Bennett
**Layout:** Grzegorz Madejak
**Production Operations Manager:** Katie Bennett
**Publishing Technology Manager:** Rebeka Davies
**Head of Publishing:** Sarah Clark
**Photography Credits:** iStock 14TL, 14TL, 15M, 15, 15T, 16ML, 16ML; Public domain 26; Shutterstock 1, 4, 5, 7, 9, 10, 12, 14ML, 15M, 15M, 14M, 15T, 16TL, 16MC, 18TL, 18ML, 18MC, 18ML, 20TL, 20ML, 20MC, 20ML, 22, 23, 24, 27, 28, 29, 30, 32, 35, 37, 38, 39, 41, 42, 45, 46, 47, 48, 49, 50, 51, 52, 53, 54, 55, 56, 57, 58, 60, 63, 65, 67, 69, 71, 73, 74, 75, 76, 77, 78, 79, 80, 82, 84, 85, 87, 89, 90, 92, 95, 96, 97, 98, 99, 100, 101, 102, 103, 104, 105, 107, 109, 110, 111, 113, 114
**Cover Credits:** Black lake in Durmitor National Park **Shutterstock**

## About the author

Marc Di Duca has been a travel guide author for 20 years and has contributed to over 150 guides for all major travel publishers. He has covered destinations as diverse as Siberia and the Caribbean but is based in the beautiful spa town of Mariánské Lázně in the Czech Republic where he lives with his Ukrainian wife Tanya and their two sons.

This book builds on original content by Rudolf Abraham.

**Distribution**
**UK, Ireland and Europe:** Apa Publications (UK) Ltd; sales@roughguides.com
**United States and Canada:** Ingram Publisher Services; ips@ingramcontent.com
**Australia and New Zealand:** Booktopia; retailer@booktopia.com.au
**Worldwide:** Apa Publications (UK) Ltd; sales@roughguides.com

**Special Sales, Content Licensing and CoPublishing**
Rough Guides can be purchased in bulk quantities at discounted prices. We can create special editions, personalised jackets and corporate imprints tailored to your needs. sales@roughguides.com; http://roughguides.com



Printed in Czech Republic

This book was produced using **Typefi** automated publishing software.



## Contact us

Every effort has been made to provide accurate information in this publication, but changes are inevitable. The publisher cannot be held responsible for any resulting loss, inconvenience or injury sustained by any traveller as a result of information or advice contained in the guide. We would appreciate it if readers would call our attention to any errors or outdated information, or if you feel we've left something out. Please send your comments with the subject line "Rough Guide Mini Montenegro Update" to mail@uk.roughguides.com.